THE FUNNIEST GUY IN THE ROOM

A BOOK OF INAPPROPRIATE HUMOR

BY STEVE CASE

THE APOCRYPHILE PRESS
BERKELEY, CA

apocryphile press
BERKELEY, CA

Apocryphile Press
1700 Shattuck Ave #81
Berkeley, CA 94709
www.apocryphile.org

Printed in the United States of America
ISBN 9781940671802

THE FUNNIEST GUY IN THE ROOM

A BOOK OF INAPPROPRIATE HUMOR

an Introduction by the Archangel Gabriel

Mostly, I knew his mother. I think that's where he got his sense of humor. His step-dad could work up a laugh now and then. Big guy, carpenter. Mostly serious though. His real Dad? Well, we're talking about the being who created laughter in the first place. Hard not to talk about heredity. But his mother was quick...Jesus got that from her.

I "appeared" to her when she was just a kid and did the whole "Fear not" speech. Her reaction was exactly what you would expect. They seriously cleaned that up for the book. I mean what would you say? Jesus' humor was mostly old-school. He could zing the Pharisees with a pithy one-liner, but he liked the old school stuff.

There was one time when he was coming home...it was going to be his first time on stage and Mary (no not that one, his Mom. Believe me that got awkward sometimes, too.) His mother had told the whole town her boy was coming home. I mean she told EVERYbody. The place was packed, and Jesus walks out there and starts his act. Nothing. I mean, total crickets. Then he starts in with the Son of God stuff. Didn't even really ease into it. I think he felt it going south and panicked. It was over pretty quickly after that. You want to talk about hecklers. These people tried to throw him off a cliff.

After that, he did a lot of his routines down near the beach. No cliffs, right? Sometimes he'd get in a boat and row a bit away from shore and do his stand-up in the boat. People thought it was his gimmick. That was where he started building his entourage. Jim and John, the Fisher brothers. Peter, of course. Matthew was the booking agent. Jesus never got involved in the money. One time he thought he'd try his hand at magic and did this incredible trick where he made a coin disappear and then reappear inside a fish. Problem was, it took so long. Peter had to go and catch the right fish and by that time half the crowd had wandered away.

When you give someone laughs like that, when you give them humor that comes from your soul and lifts theirs up... you don't forget that.

Later, he was filling stadiums. Four or five thousand people, easy. The size of the crowd never bothered him. Neither did his critics, and believe me, he had some critics. Mostly, what I think he enjoyed the most...when HE was having a good time, was when he was with his friends. The laughter just flowed out of him. Even when it was a bit they had heard a thousand times, he had a way of living in that pause before a punchline, and you couldn't help but laugh.

When you give someone laughs like that, when you give them humor that comes from your soul and lifts theirs up...you don't forget that. Every time the entourage laughed after that, they were thinking of him. They told his jokes to everyone. It just kept spreading. These people you call "gospel writers," I don't know who they were. They got a LOT of the punchlines wrong. They started worrying about whether or not the broadest audience would find it funny. They started worrying about offending the base. Nothing will kill a joke faster than that.

He's still doing the act. Old stuff and new stuff. He's been doing it for a couple of thousand years. It's a hot ticket. You get a freebie when you first get up here. Just one comp ticket, though. Best if you see him your first week here. Hard to get in, sometimes, but worth the wait.

This book is a collection of some of his best bits. This is the stuff I remember, and I was there, so I know what was said. So read on. And don't be drinking coffee when you do. I'm not cleaning that up. •

HEY JOSEPH, WHAT'S BROWN
AND SOUNDS LIKE A BELL?
I DON'T THINK THIS
IS THE TIME FOR....
DUUNNNNNNNNNG

SHEPHERD HUMOR

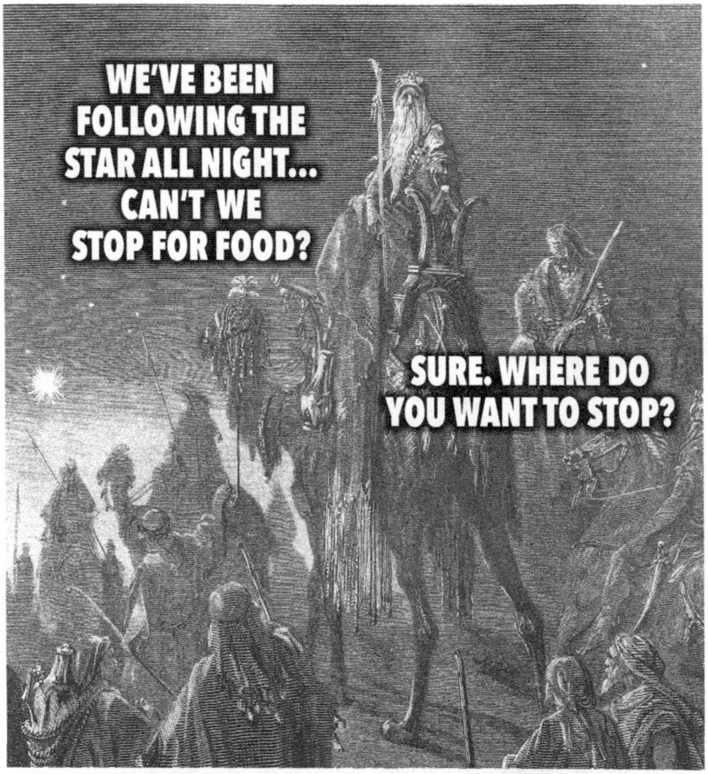
WE'VE BEEN FOLLOWING THE STAR ALL NIGHT... CAN'T WE STOP FOR FOOD?
SURE. WHERE DO YOU WANT TO STOP?

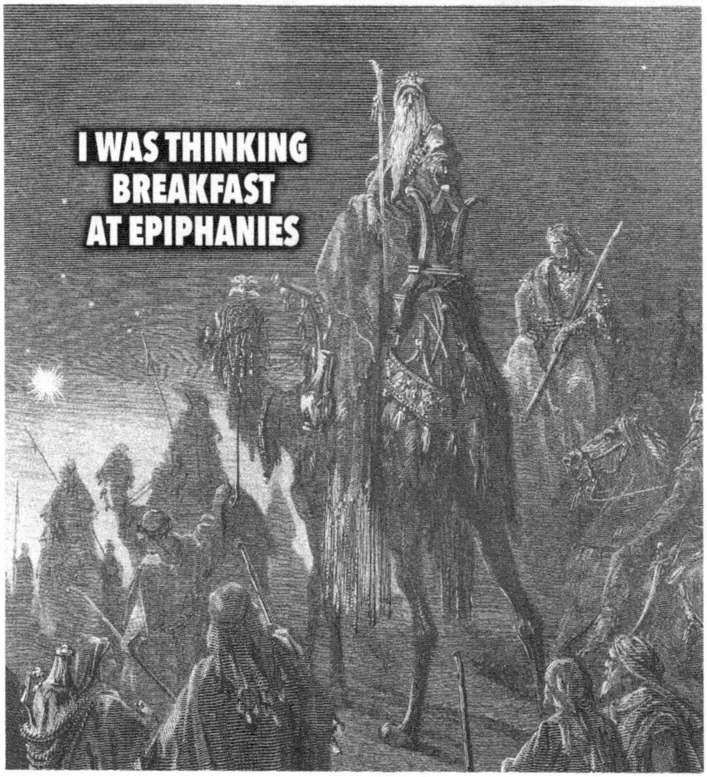
I WAS THINKING BREAKFAST AT EPIPHANIES

YOU KNOW ONLY THE CHURCH PEOPLE WILL GET THAT ONE, RIGHT?

WE'VE BEEN FOLLOWING THE STAR ALL THIS TIME, AND THE SHEPHERDS GET THERE FIRST? IT'S NOT FAIR!
WELL, MAYBE WE CAN GET THE CONSTELLATION PRIZE.

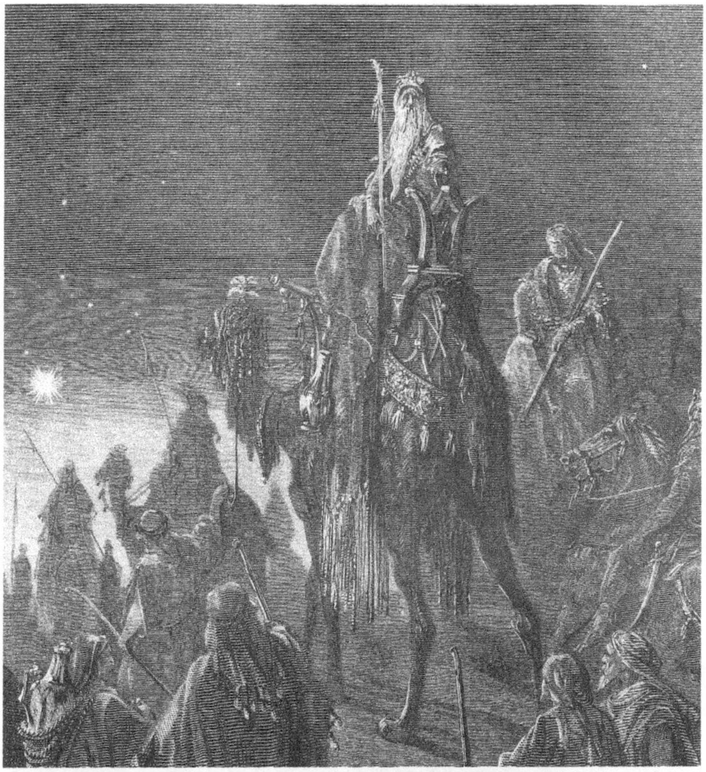

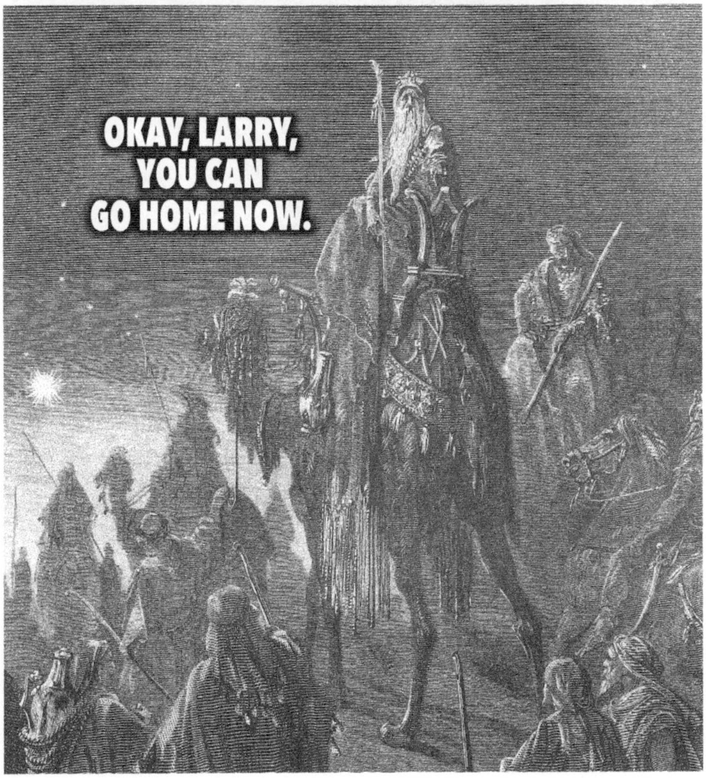
OKAY, LARRY,
YOU CAN
GO HOME NOW.

YOU KNOW, I REALLY DON'T KNOW ANYTHING ABOUT YOU.
WELL... AT ONE TIME I WAS ADDICTED TO THE HOKEY POKEY...
...BUT I TURNED MYSELF AROUND.

FRRRRRRRT

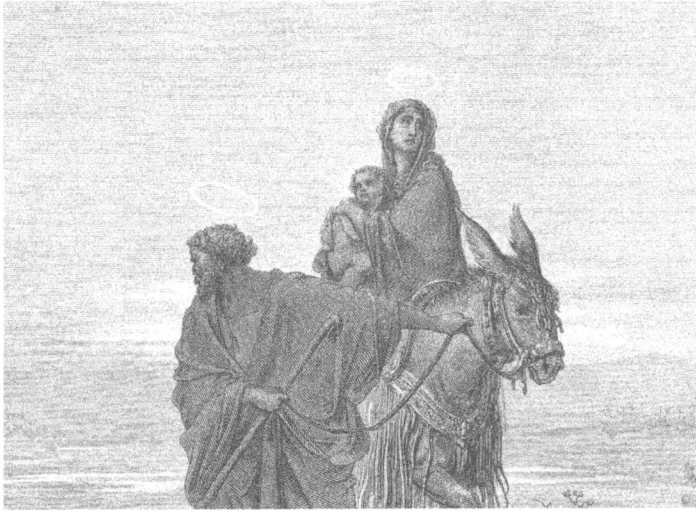

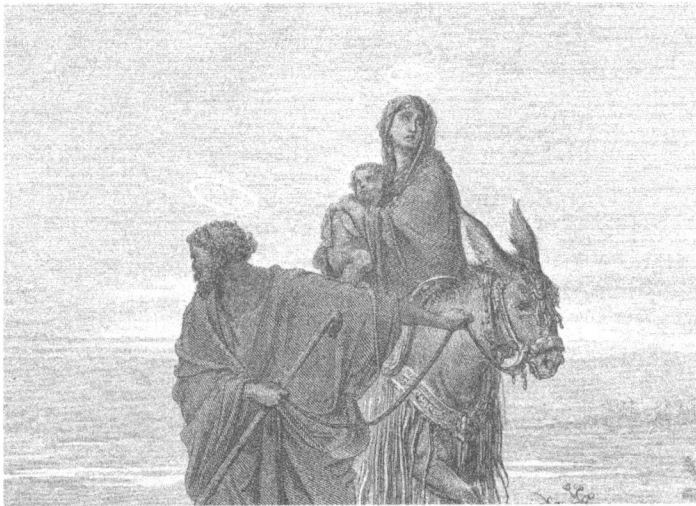

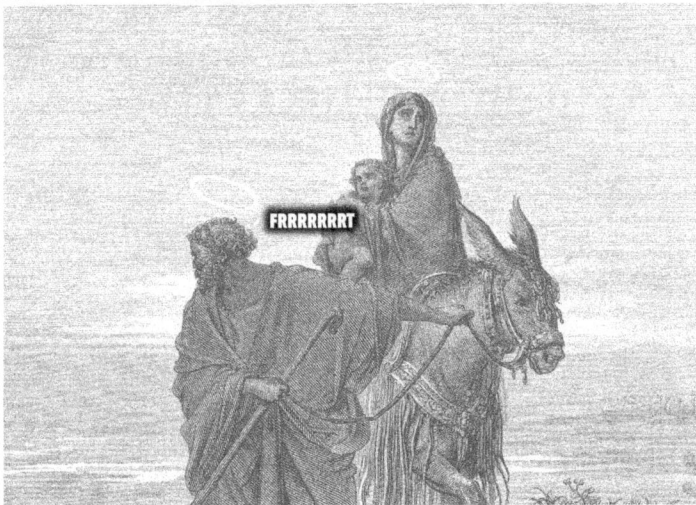

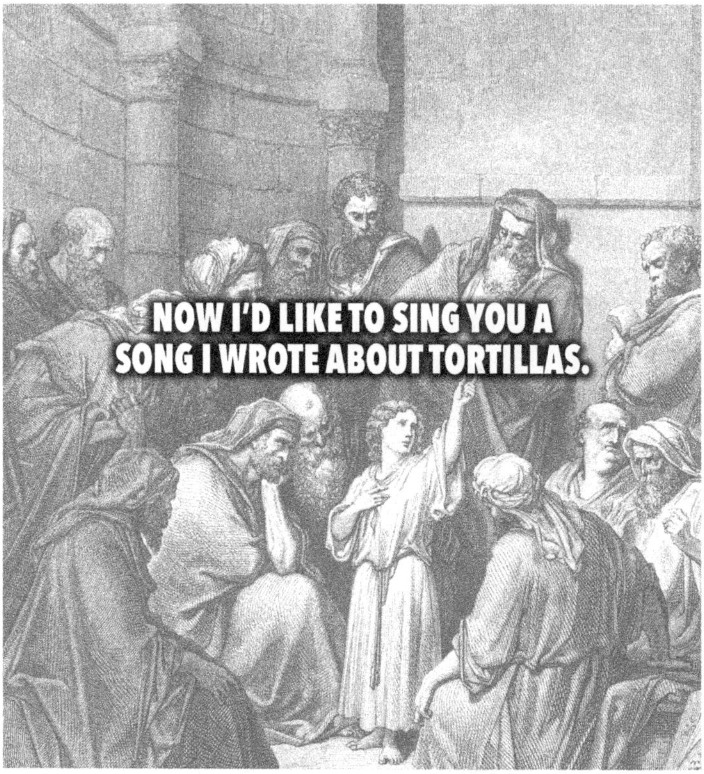
NOW I'D LIKE TO SING YOU A SONG I WROTE ABOUT TORTILLAS.

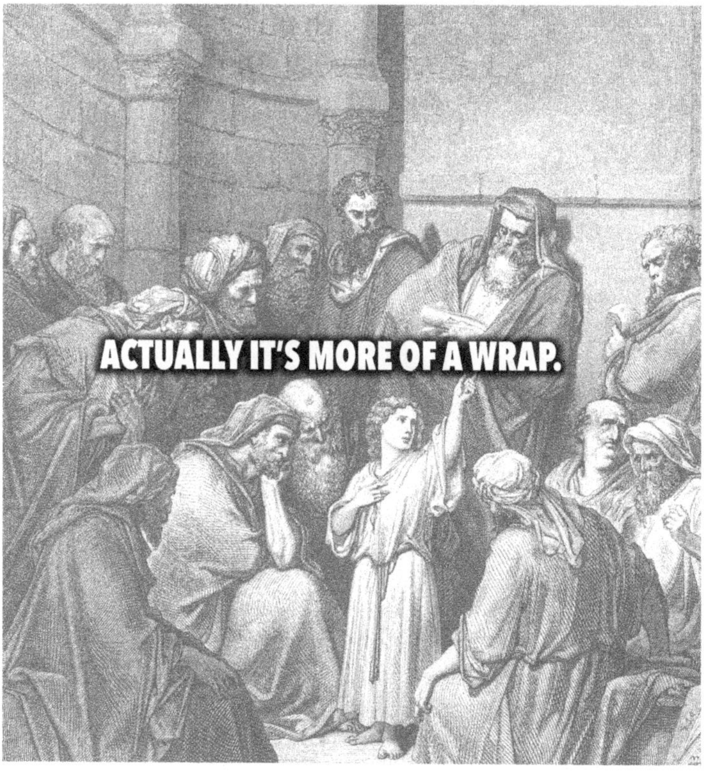
ACTUALLY IT'S MORE OF A WRAP.

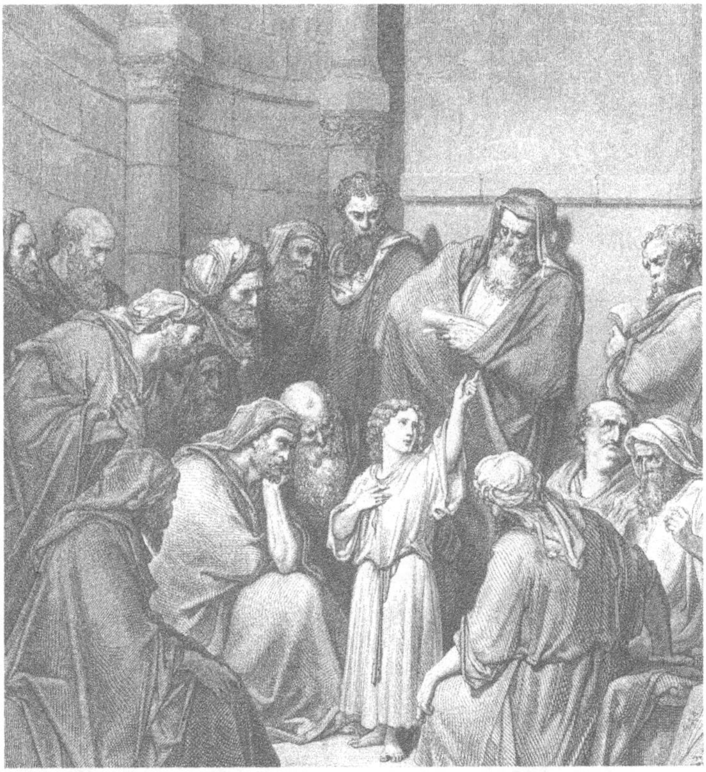

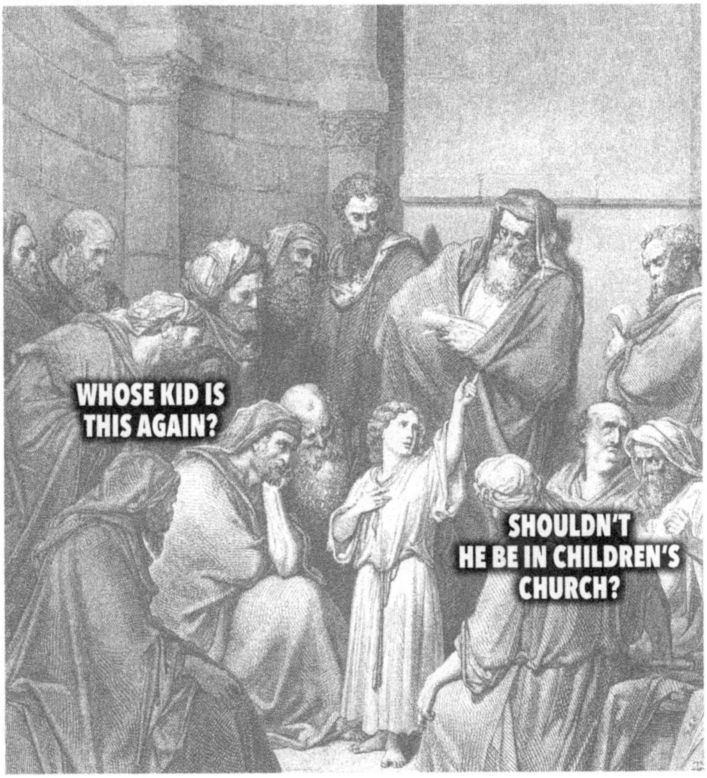
WHOSE KID IS
THIS AGAIN?
SHOULDN'T
HE BE IN CHILDREN'S
CHURCH?

HEY JESUS, WHAT DID THE GREEN GRAPE SAY TO THE PURPLE GRAPE?
NOT NOW, MATTHEW.
BREATHE YOU IDIOT! BREATHE!

'CAUSE THE GRAPE WAS PURPLE, THE GREEN GRAPE THOUGHT...
OKAY, JUDAS. YOU'RE UP.

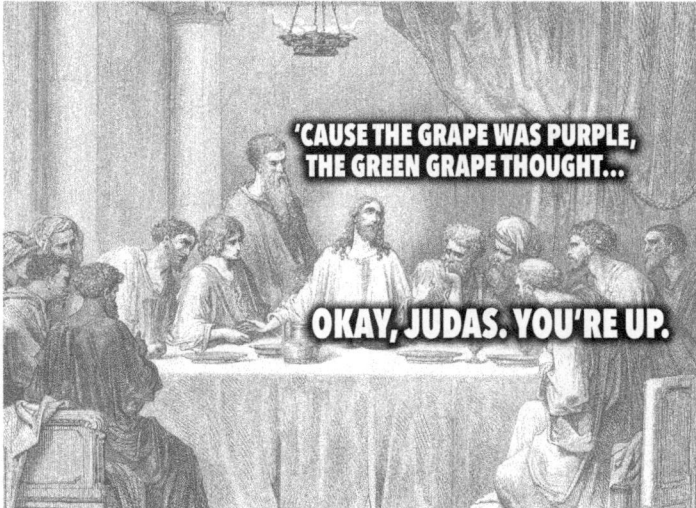

YOU KNOW THE WEDDING IN CANA WAS A VERY EMOTIONAL EXPERIENCE.
REALLY?

YES, EVEN THE CAKE WAS IN TIERS.

THE CAKE WAS IN TIERS, PETER.
STOP TALKING TO ME, JESUS.

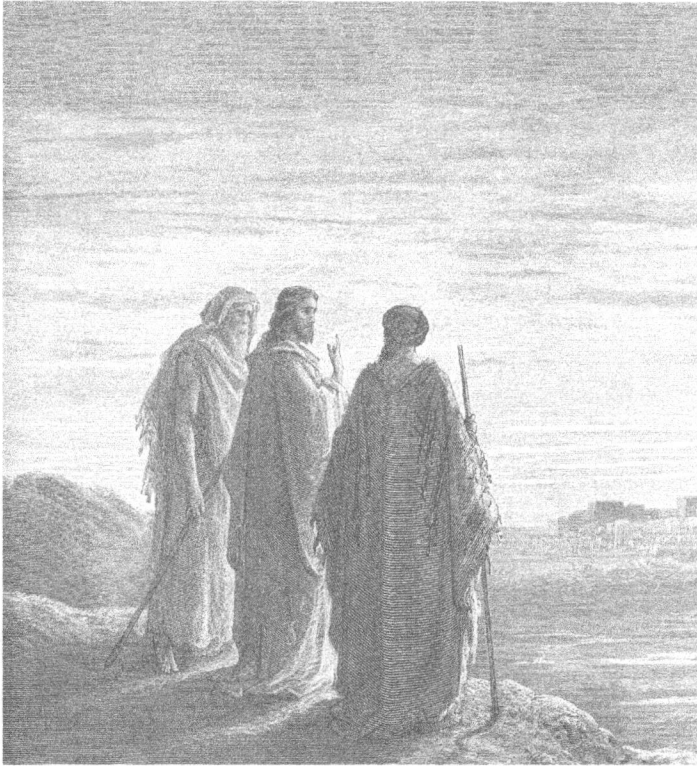

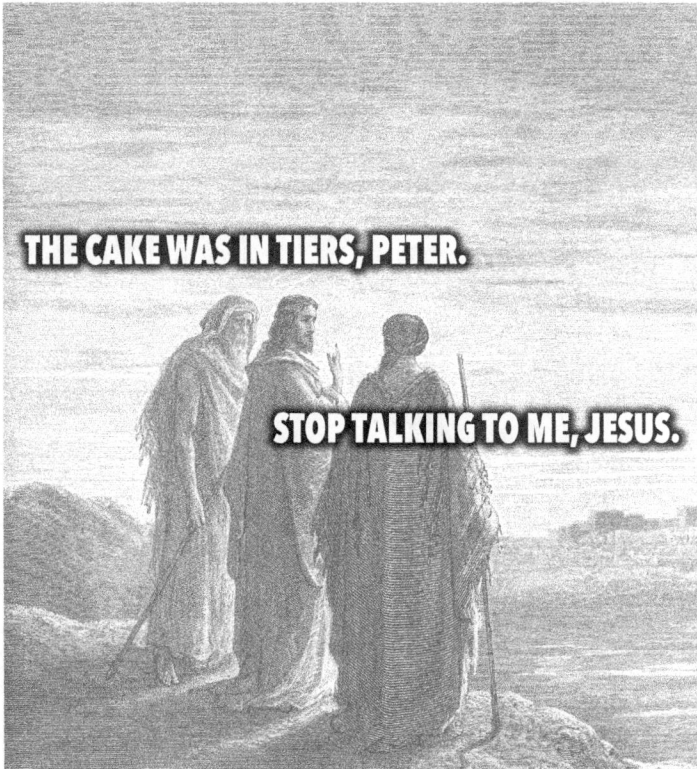

YOU REMEMBER MY SISTER, DON'T YOU? SHE'S A VEGETARIAN.
NO, I NEVER MET HERBIVORE.

YOU KNOW, JESUS, I DON'T CARE WHAT YOUR MOTHER SAYS, YOU'RE REALLY NOT ALL THAT FUNNY.

I COULD SURE GO FOR QUESADILLA ABOUT NOW.
WHY DON'T YOU START WITH ONE DILLA AND SEE HOW YOU FEEL?

ONE DILLA, JESUS
GOD, I HATE STAFF LUNCH MEETINGS.

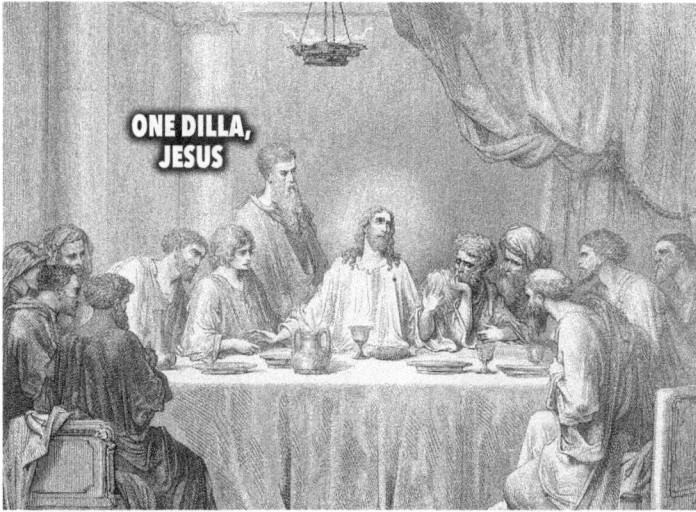

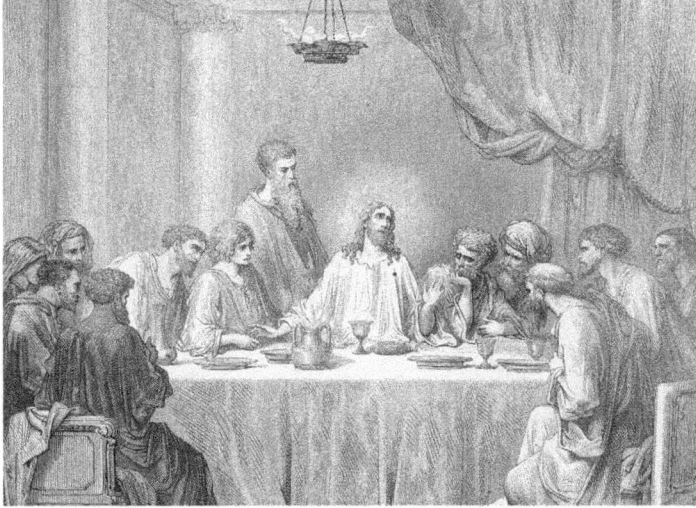

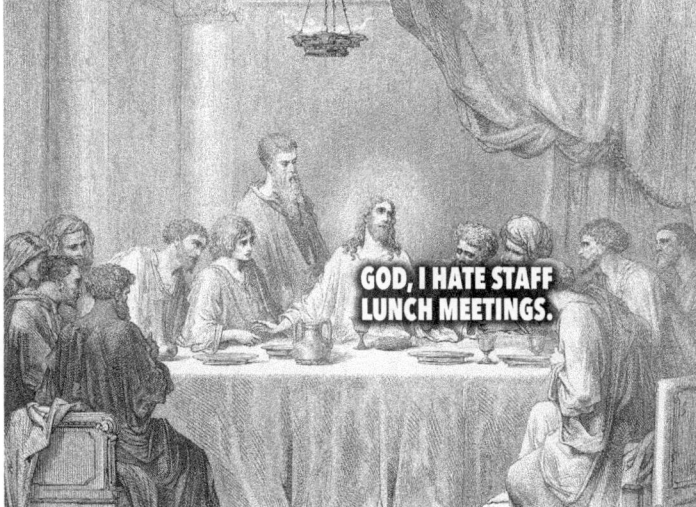

YOU KNOW, JEREMIAH WAS JUST A LITTLE FELLOW, BARELY FIVE FEET TALL.
STILL MADE SOME PRETTY GOOD MONEY.
REALLY?

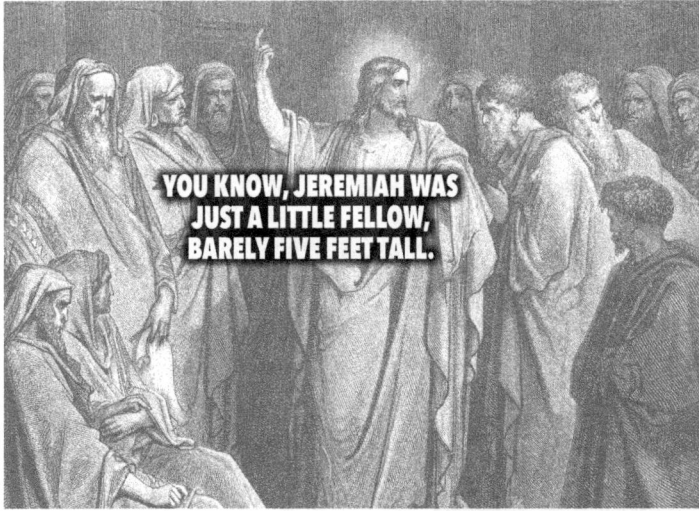

WHAT? THERE'S NOTHING WRONG WITH A LITTLE PROPHET.

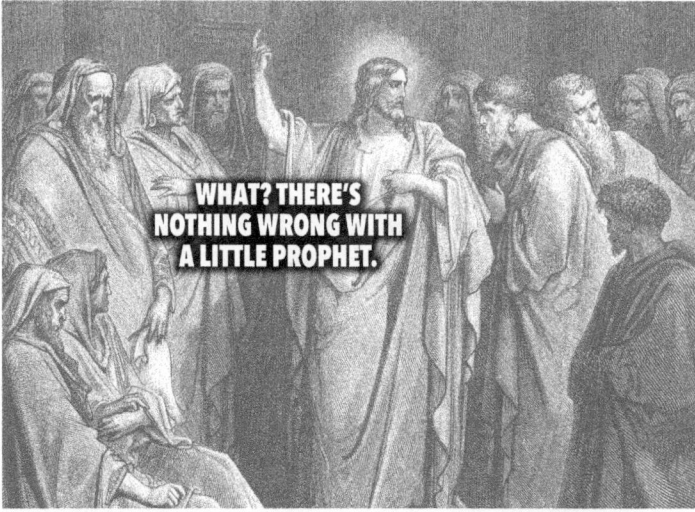

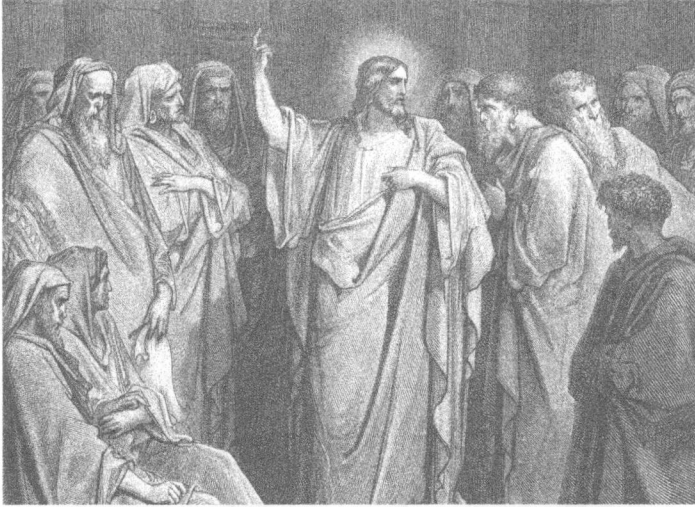

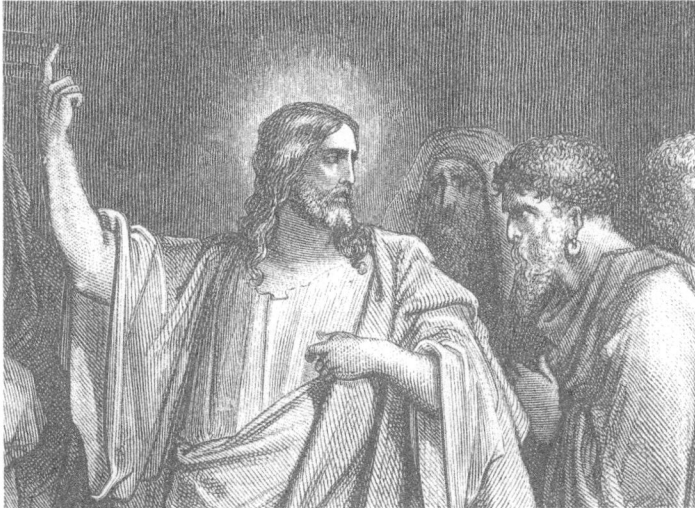

REMEMBER, ONCE WE CROSS INTO THE SERENGETI, THERE IS NO GAMBLING.
WHY NOT?
TOO MANY CHEETAHS.

TOO MANY CHEETAHS, PETER.
AND YOU WONDER WHY NOBODY WANTS TO HANG OUT WITH US.

HEY PETER,
WHAT DOES A
PIRATE SAY WHEN
HE TURNS 80?
HE SAYS,
"AYE MATEY!"

AYE MATEY, PETER.

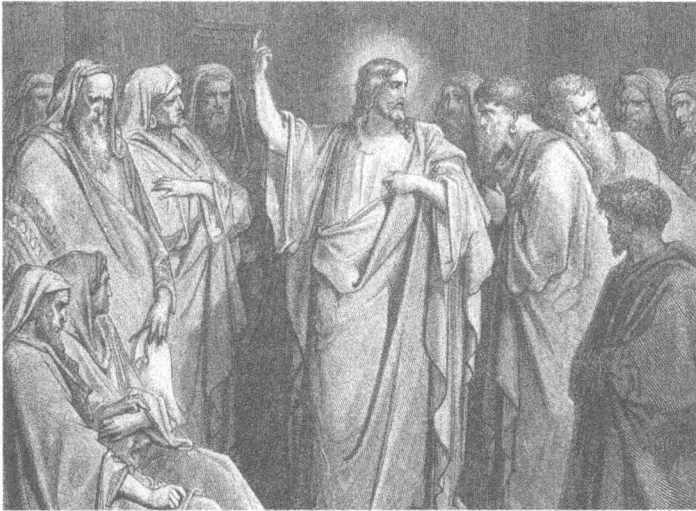

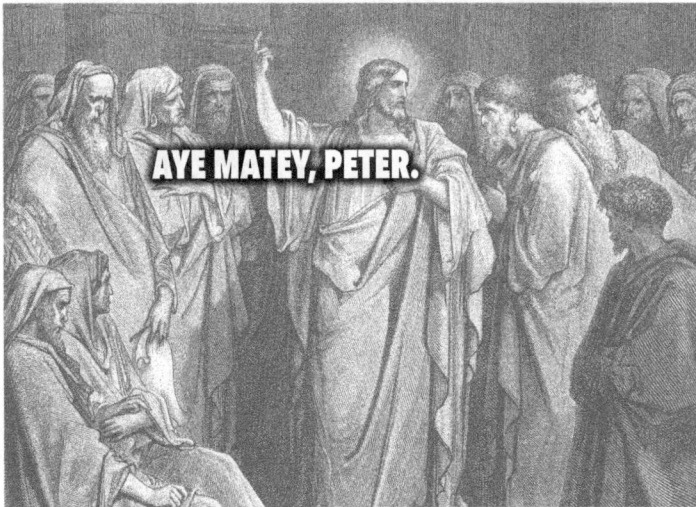

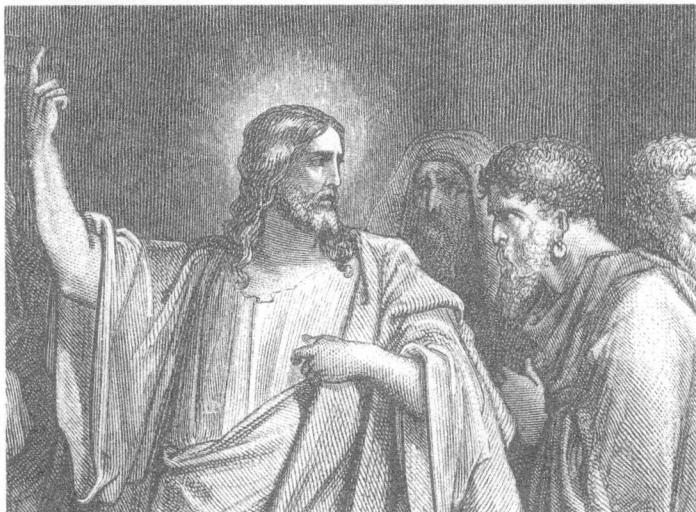

DUDE, THAT'S AN AWESOME BEARD.
THANKS. I DIDN'T LIKE IT AT FIRST...
BUT IT GREW ON ME.

IT GREW ON ME, JESUS.
YOU KNOW, SCOTT, I CAN MAKE YOU BLIND AGAIN.

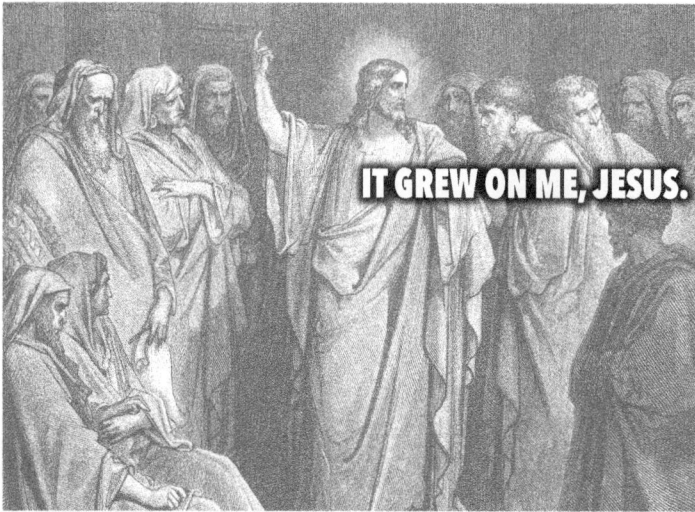

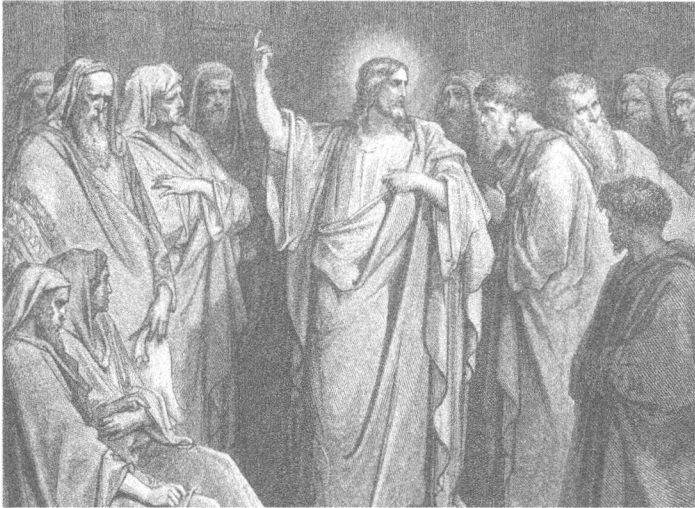

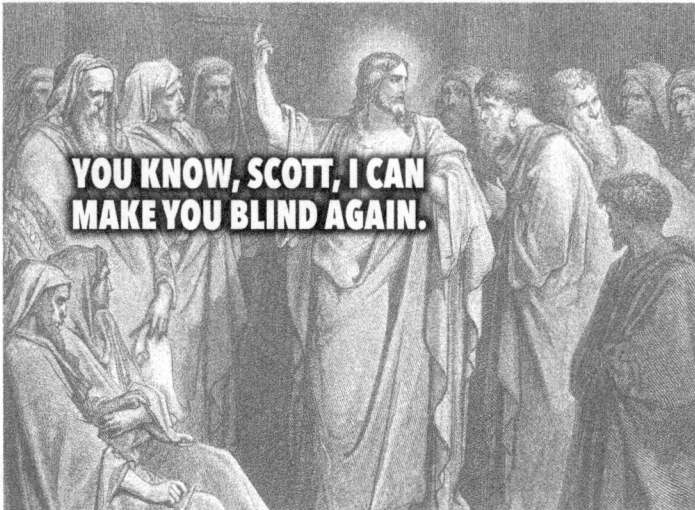

UH, MARTHA, I THINK YOU DREW YOUR EYEBROWS ON A LITTLE HIGH.
YOU LOOK SURPRISED.

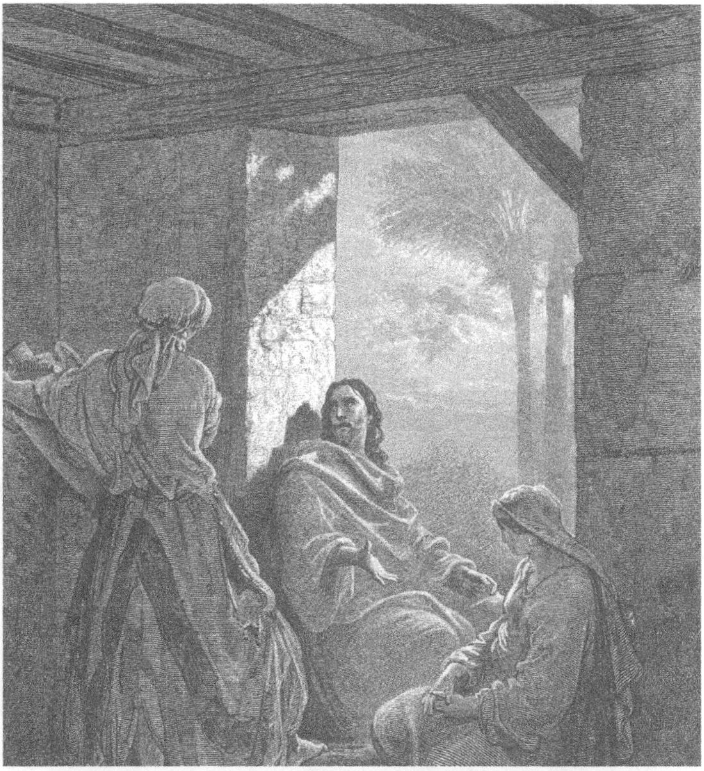

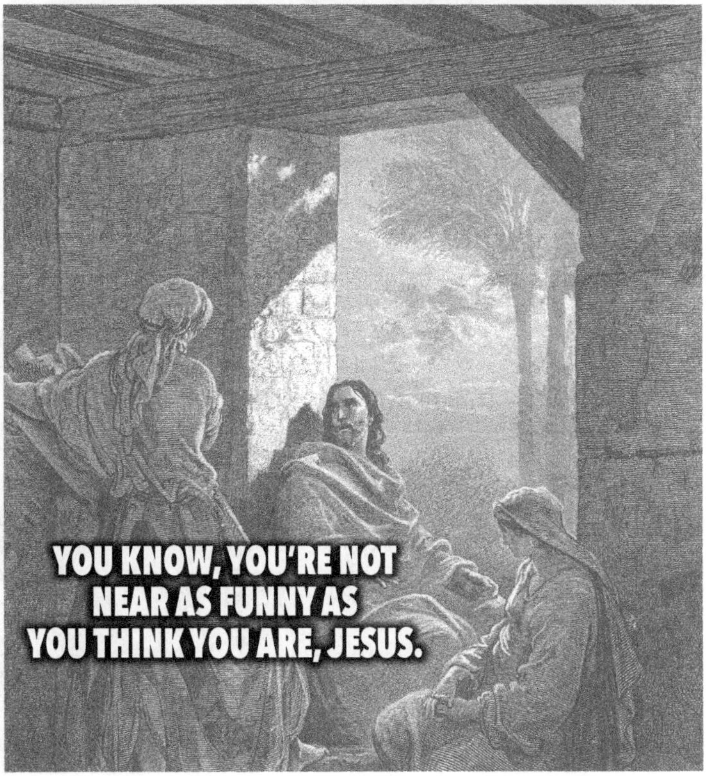
YOU KNOW, YOU'RE NOT
NEAR AS FUNNY AS
YOU THINK YOU ARE, JESUS.

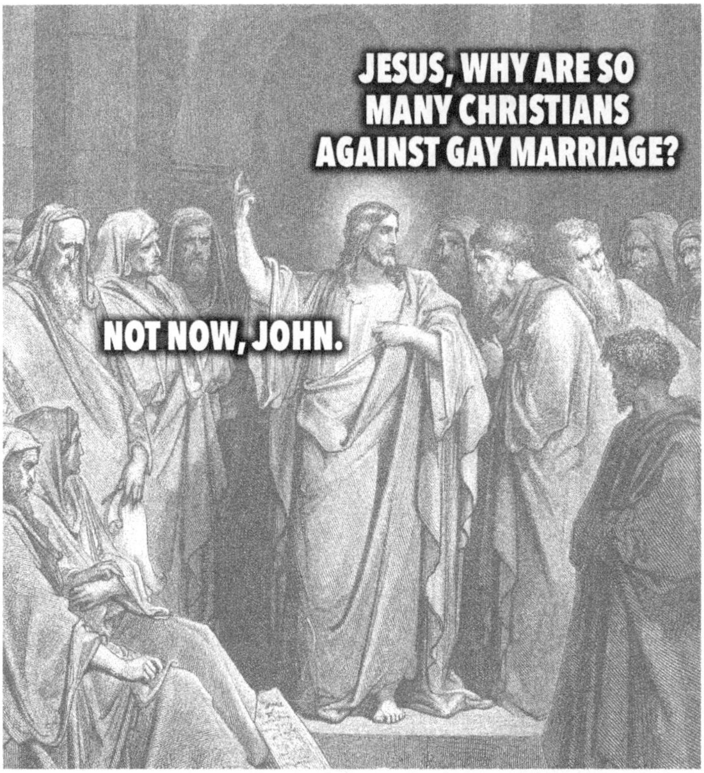
JESUS, WHY ARE SO MANY CHRISTIANS AGAINST GAY MARRIAGE?
NOT NOW, JOHN.

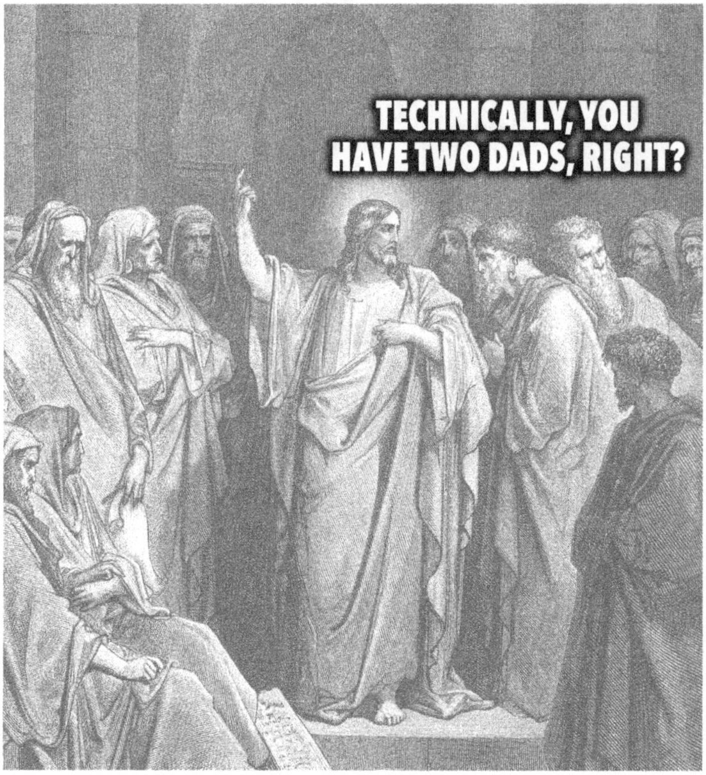
TECHNICALLY, YOU HAVE TWO DADS, RIGHT?

TWO DADS, JESUS.

HEY JESUS, HOW ARE THE NOODLES?
THEY AREN'T REAL NOODLES.
WHAT DO YOU MEAN?
THEY'RE AN IMPASTA

CHECK, PLEASE.

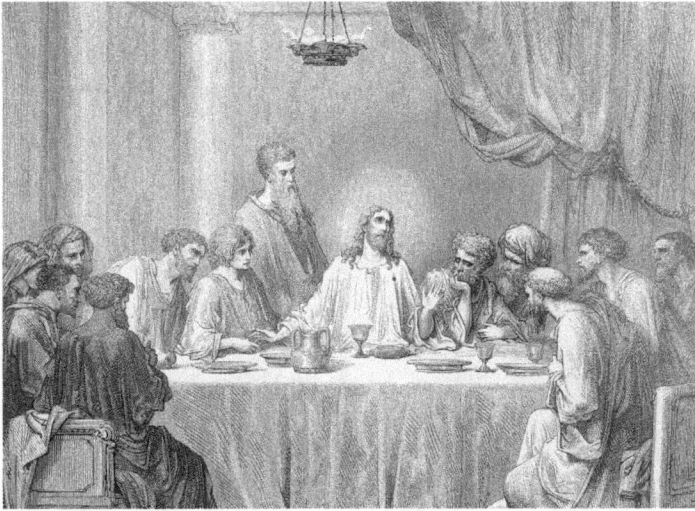

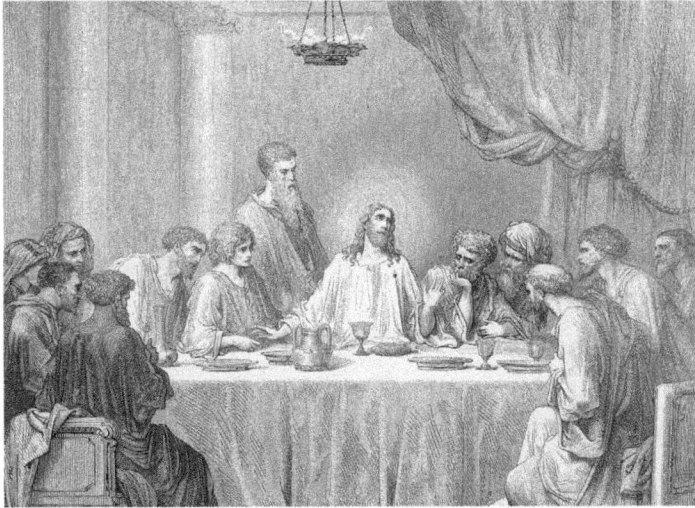

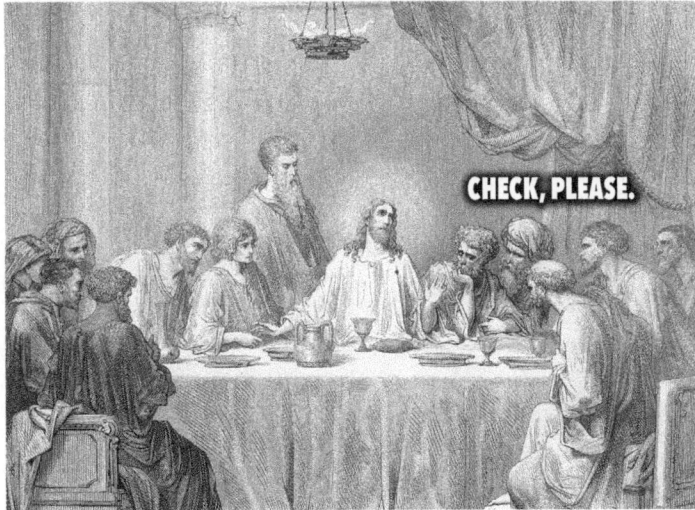

THE HOT TUB IS RIGHT OVER THERE. HELP YOURSELF.
YOU'RE SURE IT'S OKAY?
OF COURSE, IT'S SABBATH.

SEE, WHEN I SAID...NEVER MIND. GET YOUR SWIM TRUNKS.

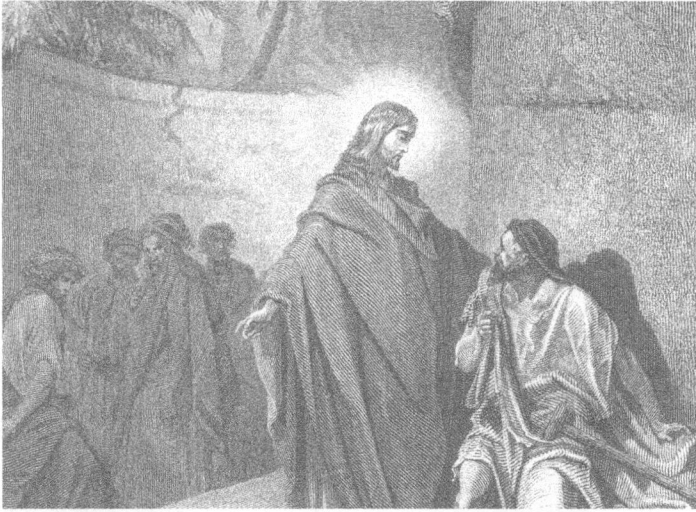

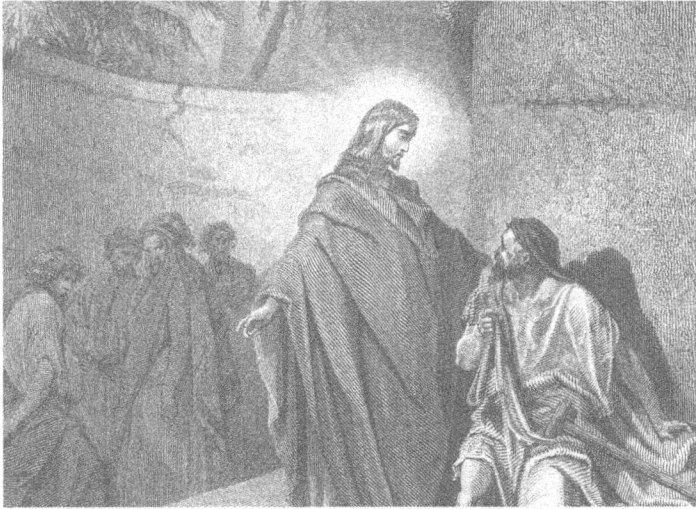

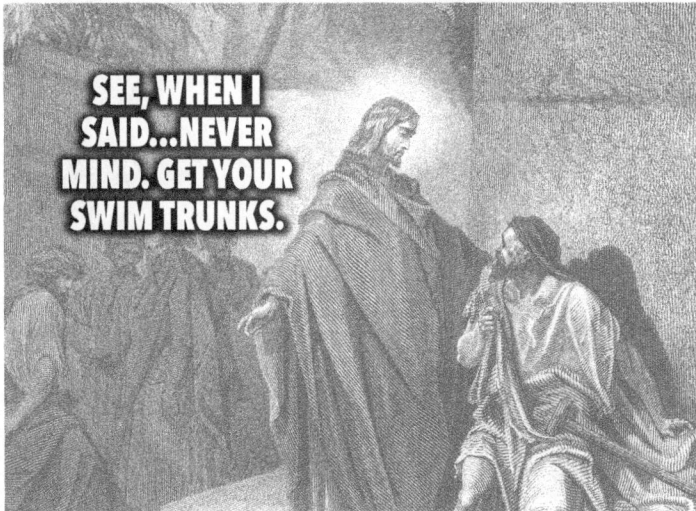

HEY JESUS, I JUST THREW YOUR DRUM AND CYMBALS OFF THE CLIFF!
BA-DUM TISSHHHHHH!

SEE, IT'S FUNNY 'CAUSE IT SOUNDS LIKE A....
SHUT UP, SATAN.

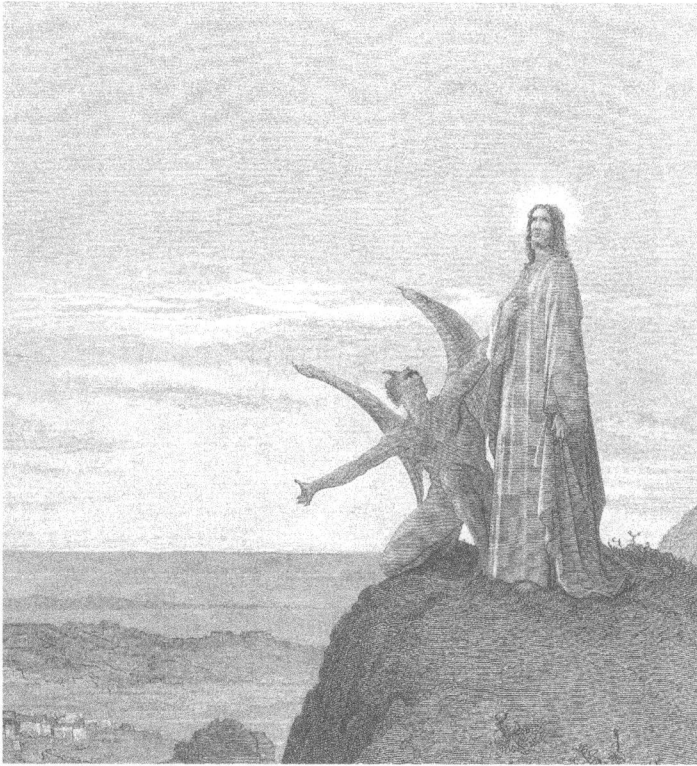

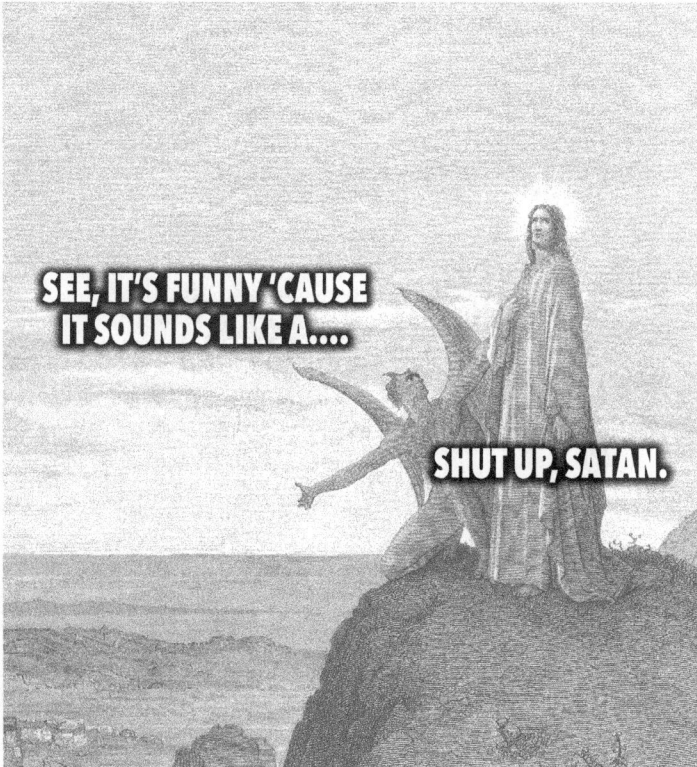

TODAY I CUT MY FINGER SHREDDING CHEESE
I THINK IT MIGHT BE A SIGN OF GRATER PROBLEMS.

HEY JOHN, PICK A COD, ANY COD!
THAT'S A REALLY STUPID JOKE, JESUS.

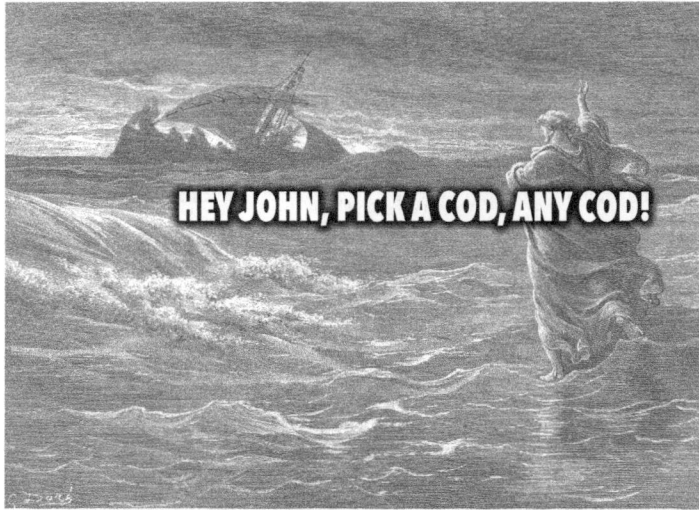

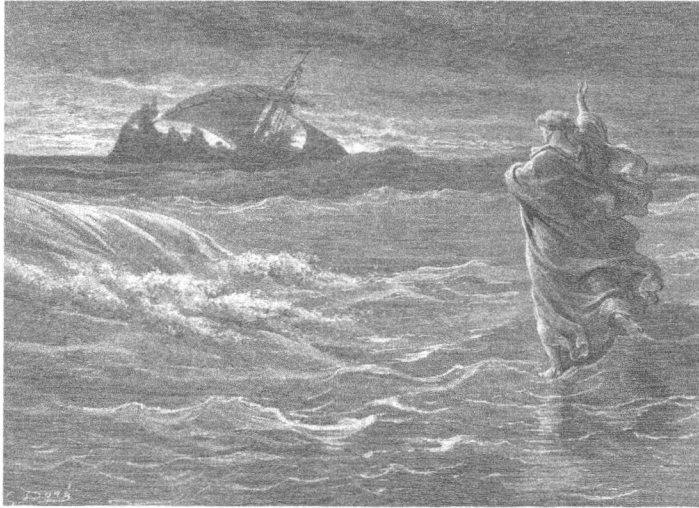

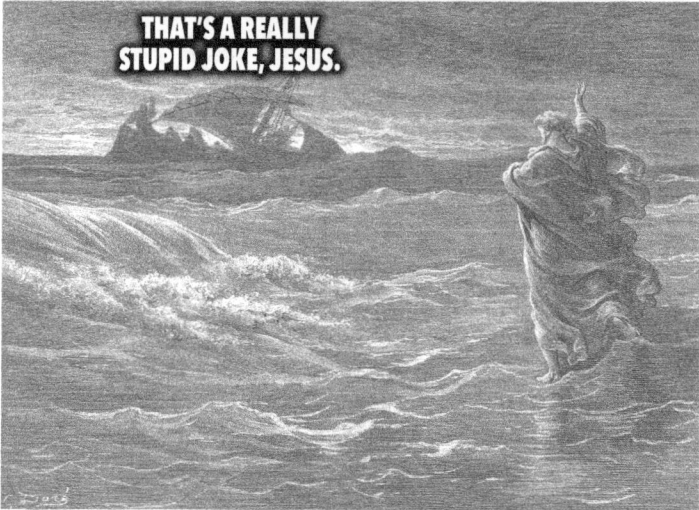

ANYTIME YOU COME UP WITH A BETTER FISH JOKE, JUST LET MINNOW.
YEAH, THAT'S WHAT I THOUGHT.

JESUS, PLEASE HEAL MY DAUGHTER. SHE'S SO COLD.
MOVE THE BED TO THE CORNER OF THE ROOM.
WHY?
BECAUSE IT'S NINETY DEGREES.

MUMMY?
HUSH. IGNORE HIM, CHILD.

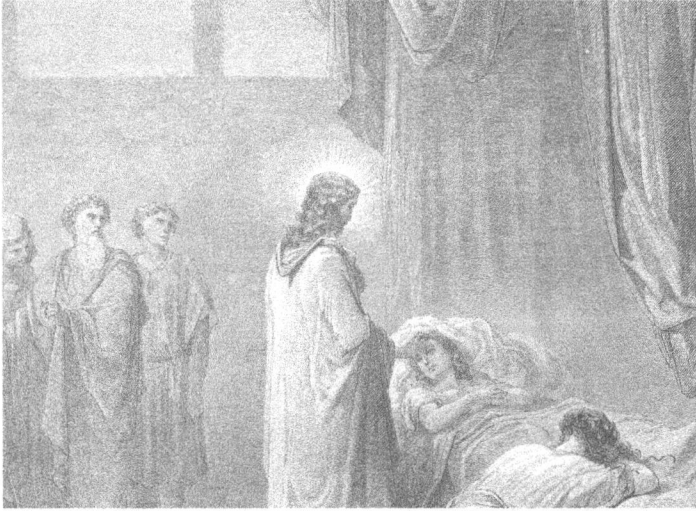

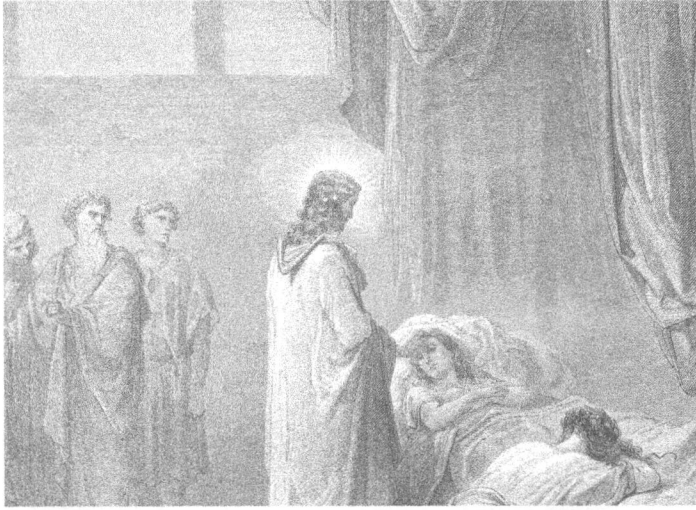

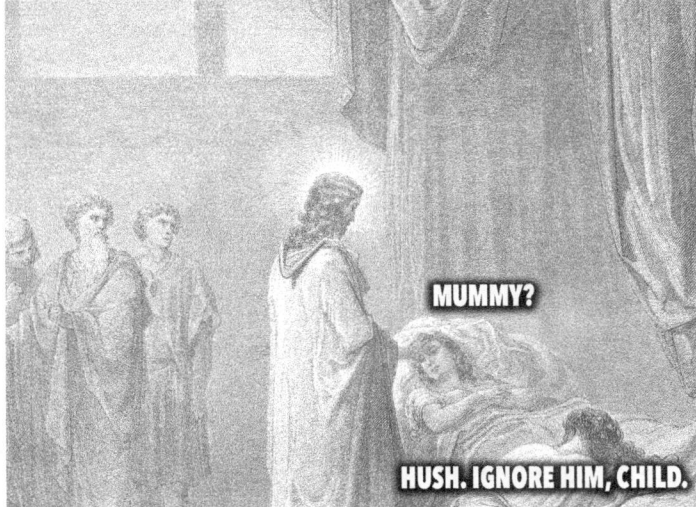

HELP HER, JESUS. SHE BROKE HER ARM IN THREE PLACES.
WELL, FIRST OF ALL, I WOULDN'T GO BACK TO THOSE PLACES.

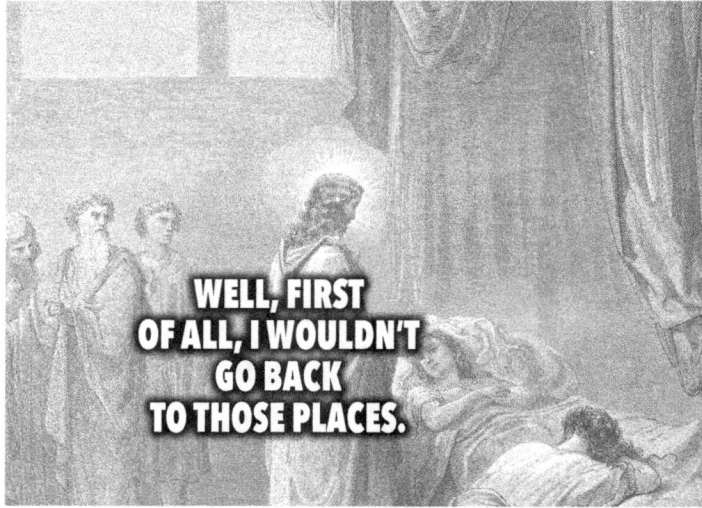

HEH
DON'T LAUGH,
HE'LL KEEP GOING.

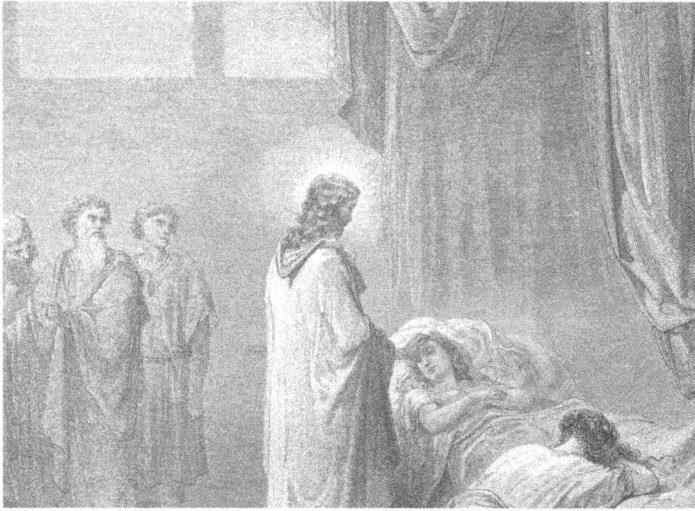

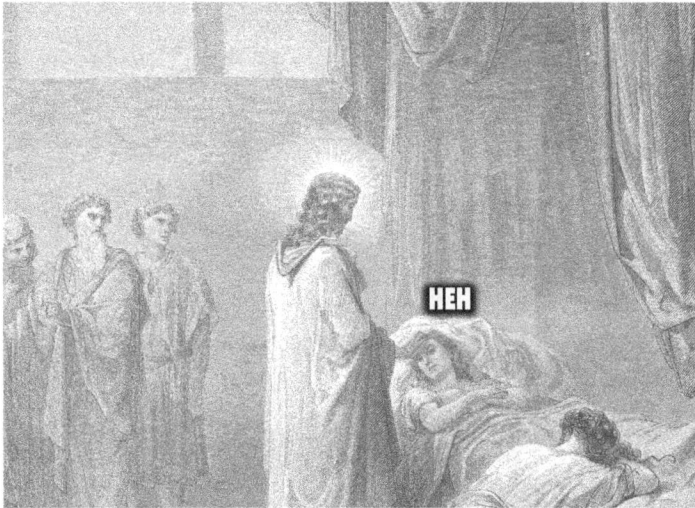

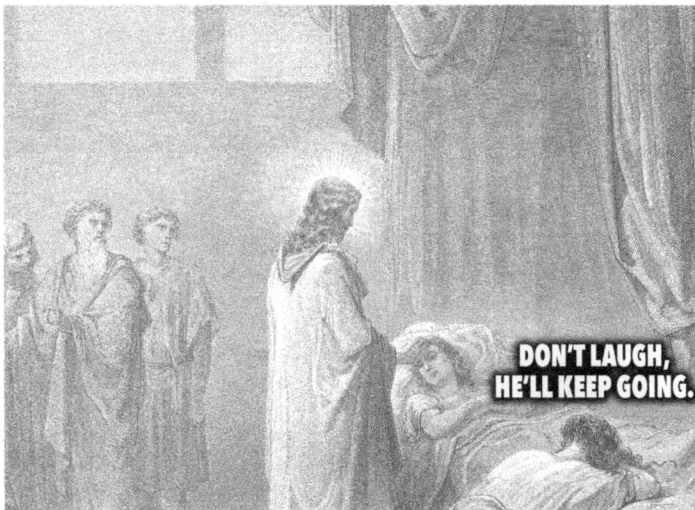

HELP HER, JESUS. SHE SAID SHE SWALLOWED A COIN.
IS SHE CHOKING?
NO, SHE REALLY DID!

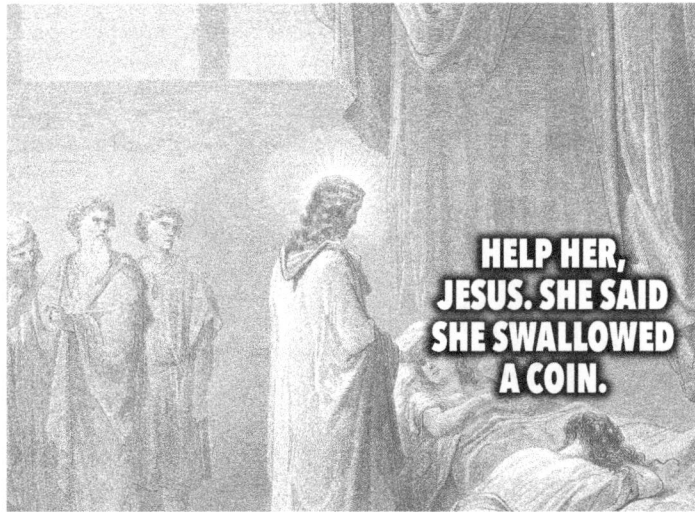

OH SHUT UP,
IT WAS MY TURN.

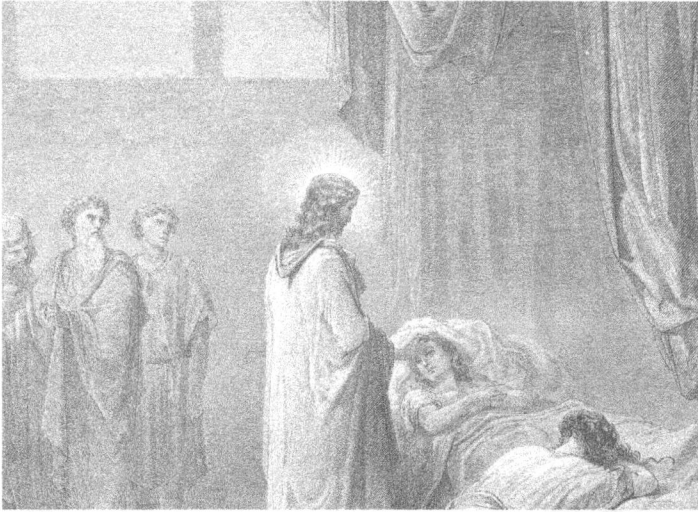

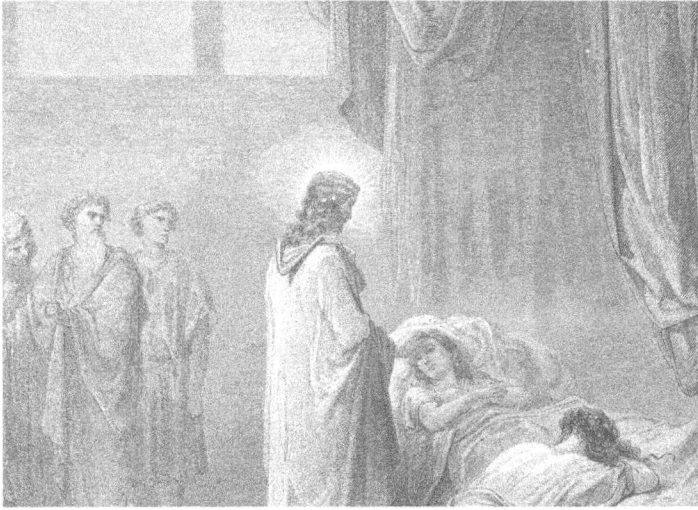

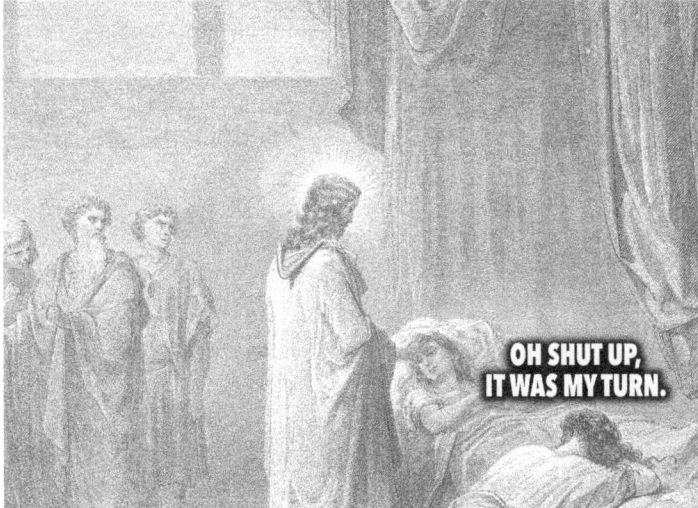

ONE TIME, MY DAD MADE A SNAIL WITHOUT A SHELL TO SEE IF IT WOULD MAKE HIM FASTER.
DID IT WORK?
NO.

IT JUST MADE HIM
A LITTLE SLUGGISH.

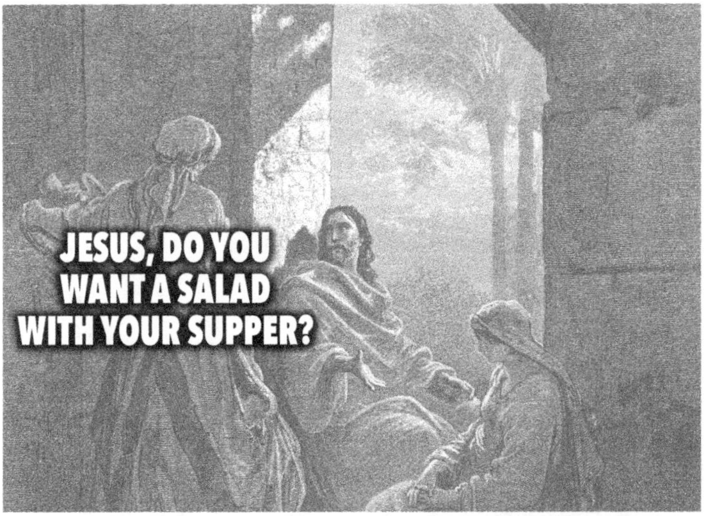
JESUS, DO YOU WANT A SALAD WITH YOUR SUPPER?

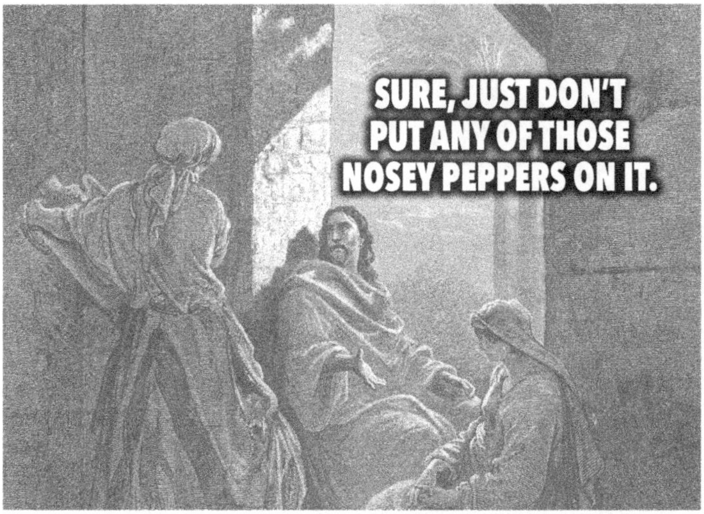
SURE, JUST DON'T PUT ANY OF THOSE NOSEY PEPPERS ON IT.

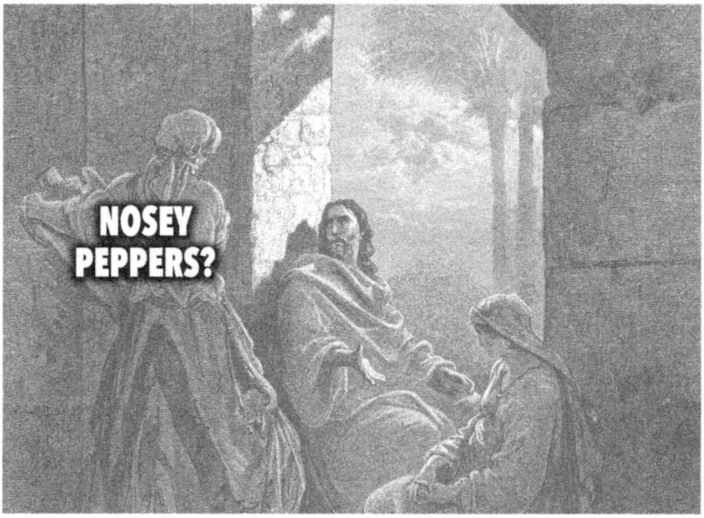
NOSEY PEPPERS?

THE ONES THAT GET JALAPENO BUSINESS.
OKAY, YOU CAN'T COME OVER ANY MORE.

HEY, PETER, PASS THE MUSTARD.
YOU JUST ASKED FOR THAT A MINUTE AGO.
WHOA, DIJON VU!

CHECK, PLEASE.

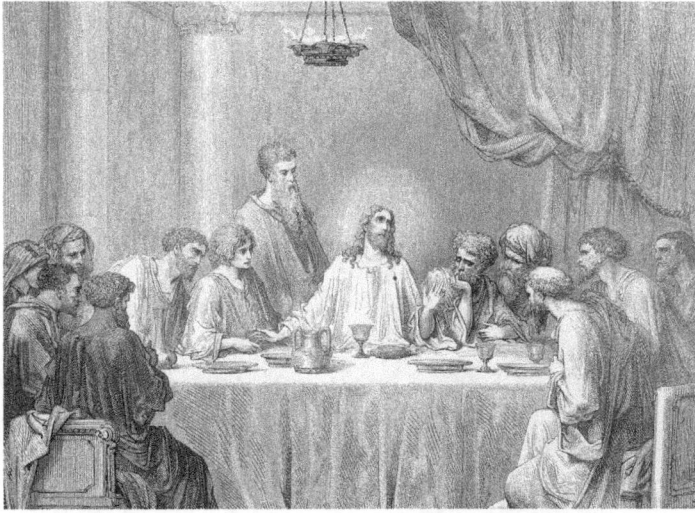

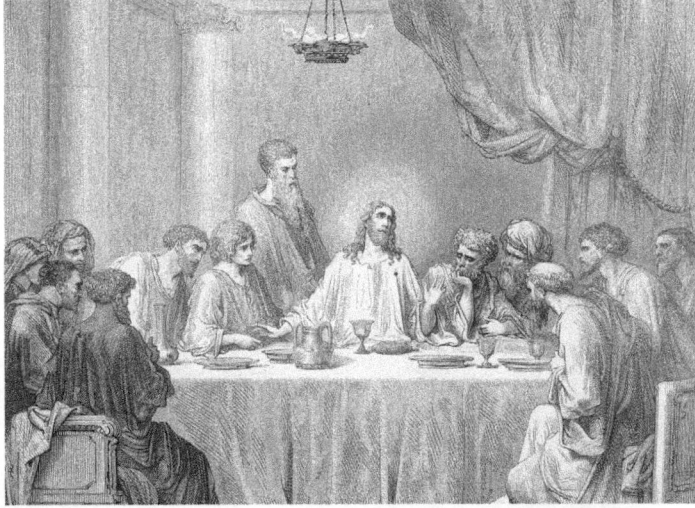

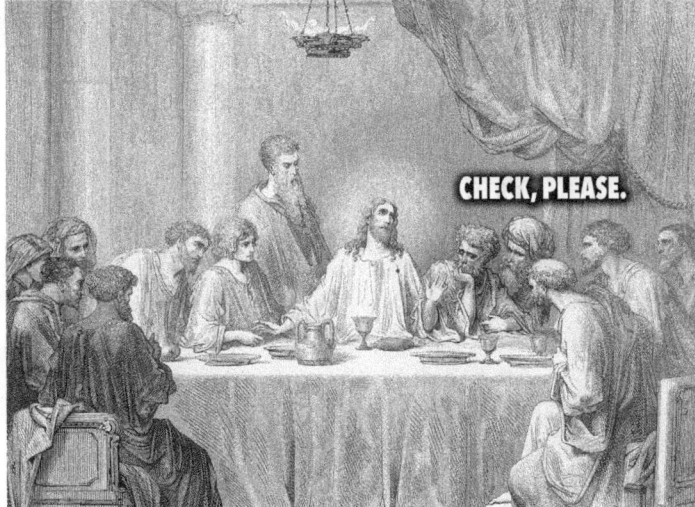

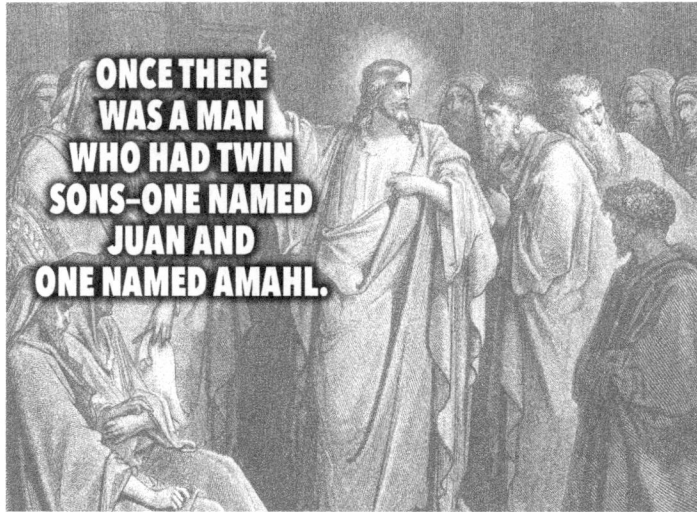

ONCE THERE WAS A MAN WHO HAD TWIN SONS—ONE NAMED JUAN AND ONE NAMED AMAHL.

AMAHL RAN AWAY FROM HOME AND SPENT HIS INERITANCE ON CHEAP LIVING.

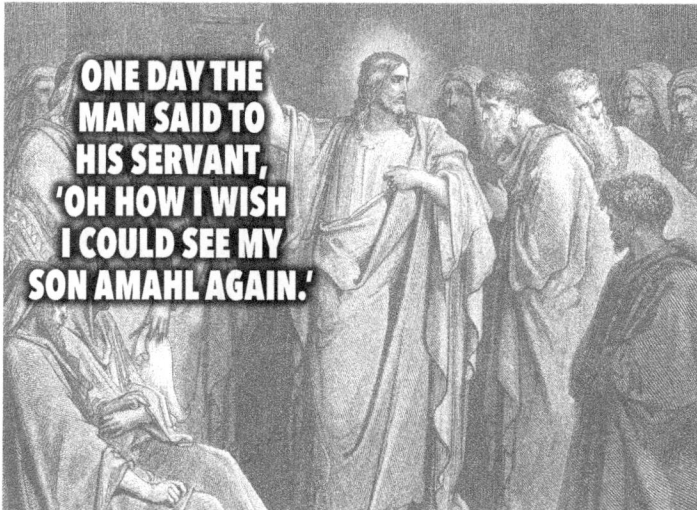

ONE DAY THE MAN SAID TO HIS SERVANT, 'OH HOW I WISH I COULD SEE MY SON AMAHL AGAIN.'

steve case presents

THE SERVANT SAID, 'THEY'RE TWINS. IF YOU'VE SEEN JUAN, YOU'VE SEEN AMAHL.'

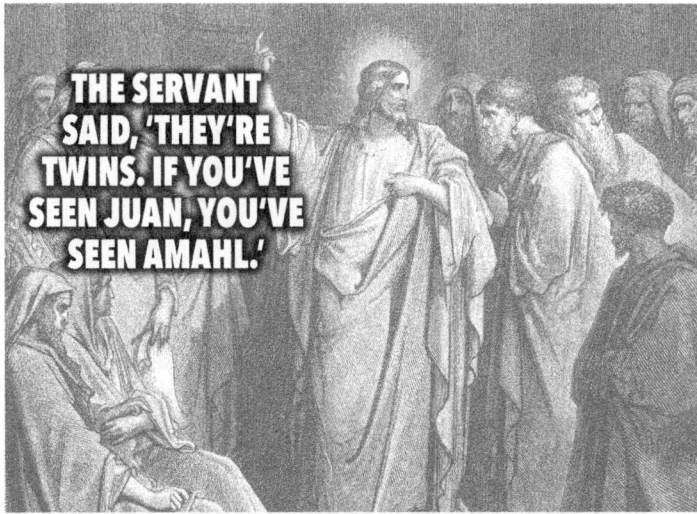

AREN'T THESE RIVER VALLEYS BEAUTIFUL, JESUS?
THEY'RE GORGES.

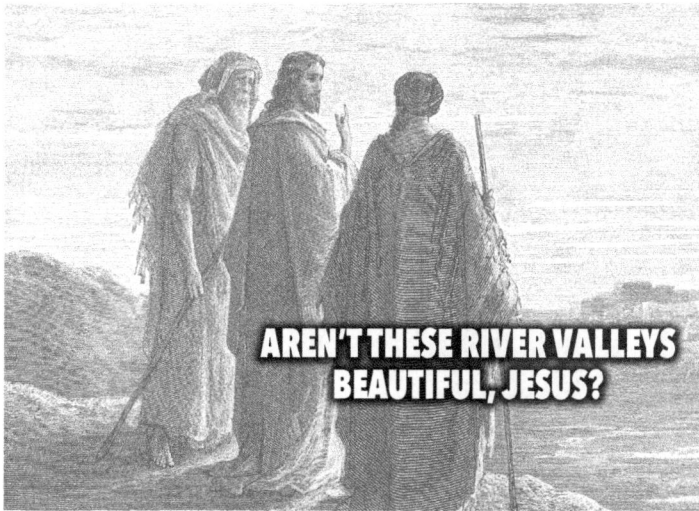

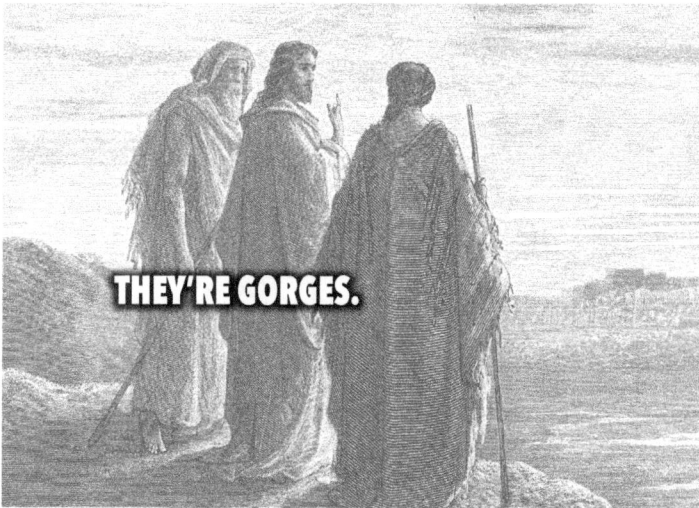

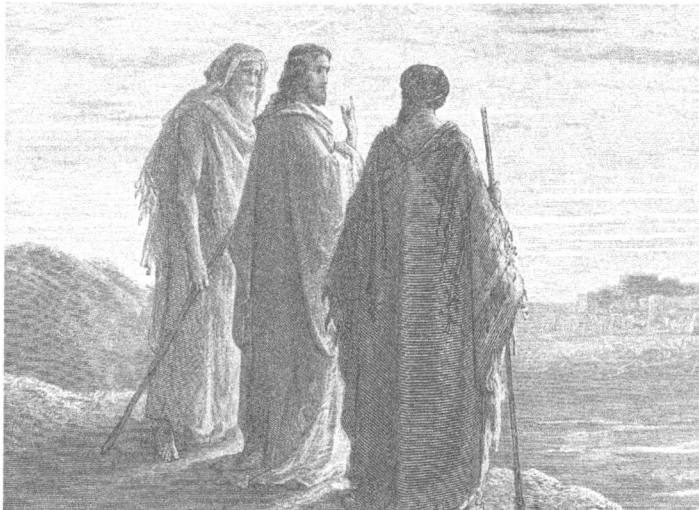

OKAY, WE'RE GOING TO PLAY THE QUIET GAME FOR THE REST OF THE TRIP.

HEY JESUS, IS IT TRUE KING DAVID WAS DYSLEXIC?
YES, SOMETIMES THE PSALMIST WROTE INVERSE.

HE WROTE INVERSE,
PETER.

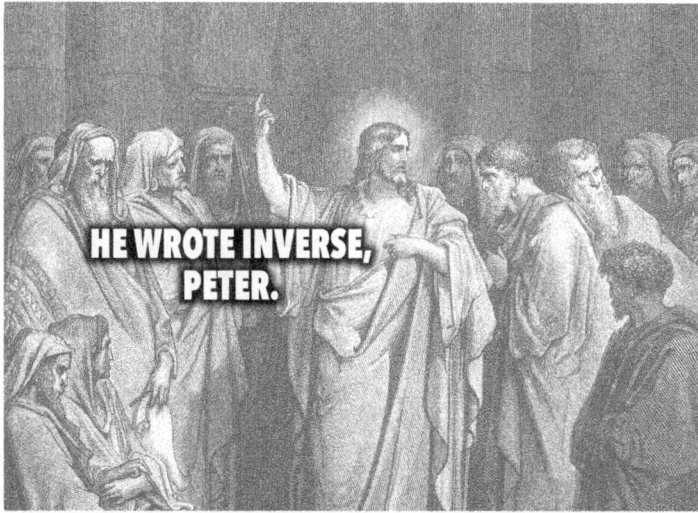

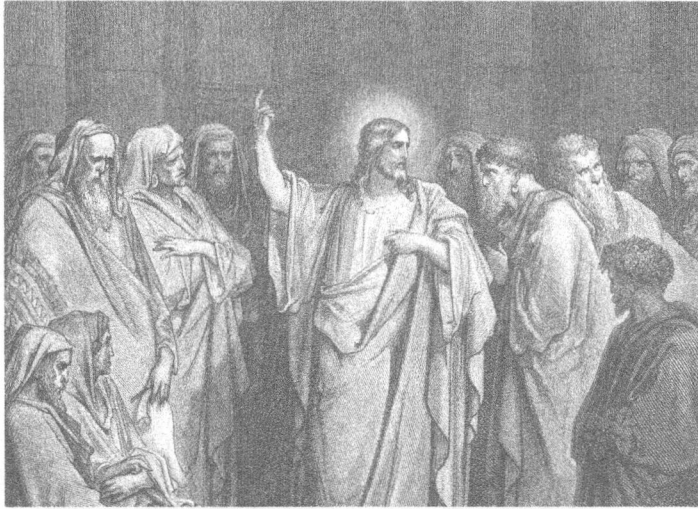

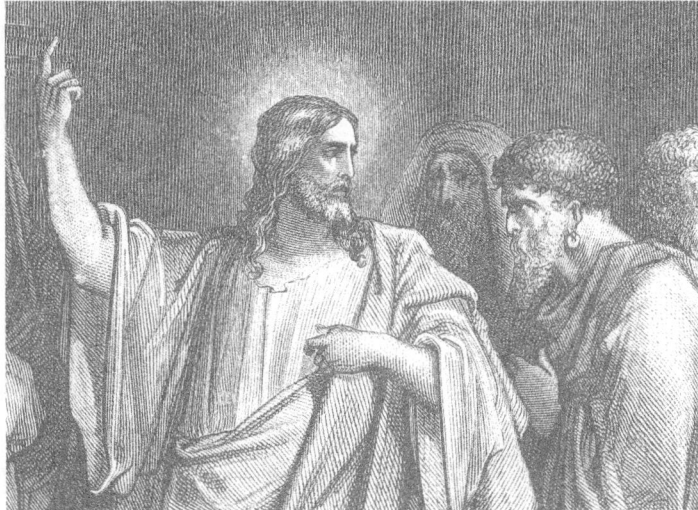

HELP HER JESUS, SHE SWALLOWED A WATCH.
WELL, THIS IS GOING TO BE TIME CONSUMING.

AND I'VE BEEN RUNNING
FAST ALL DAY.
QUIT IT.

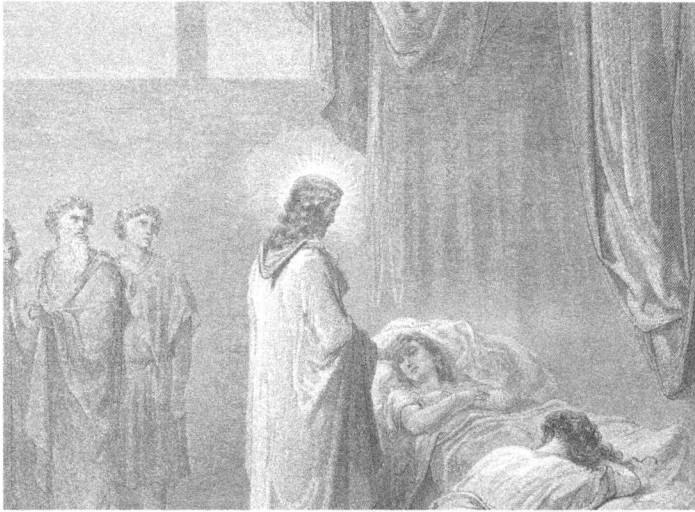

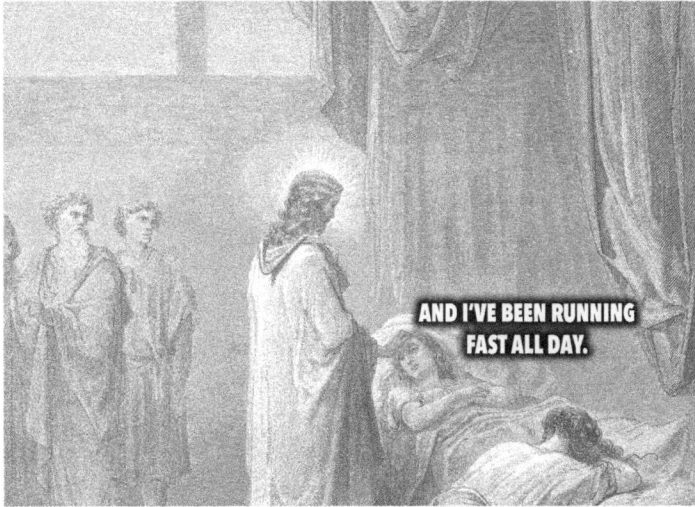

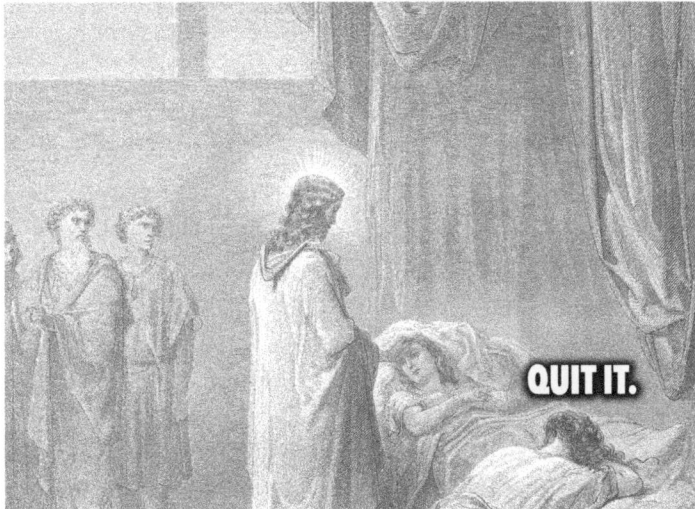

JESUS, HELP MY DAUGHTER, SHE SWALLOWED FOOD COLORING.
HOW DO YOU FEEL MY CHILD?
LIKE I DYED A LITTLE INSIDE.

SHE'S GOOD.
OH, JESUS.

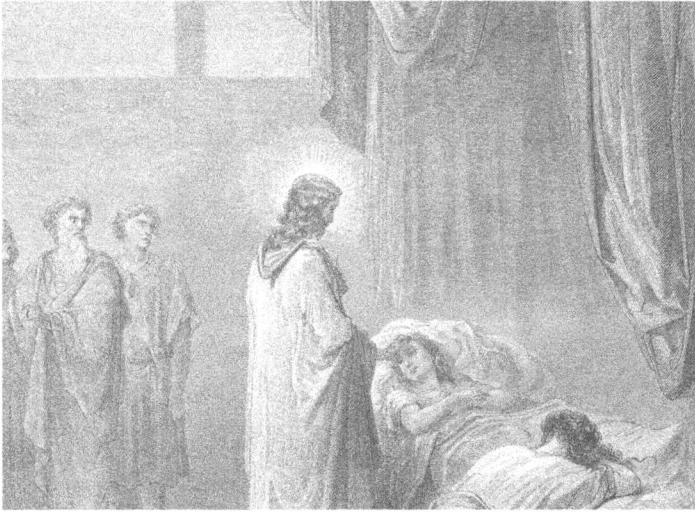

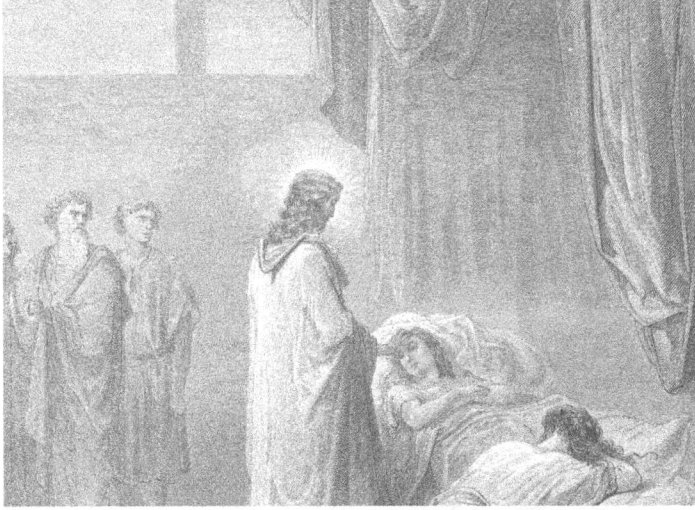

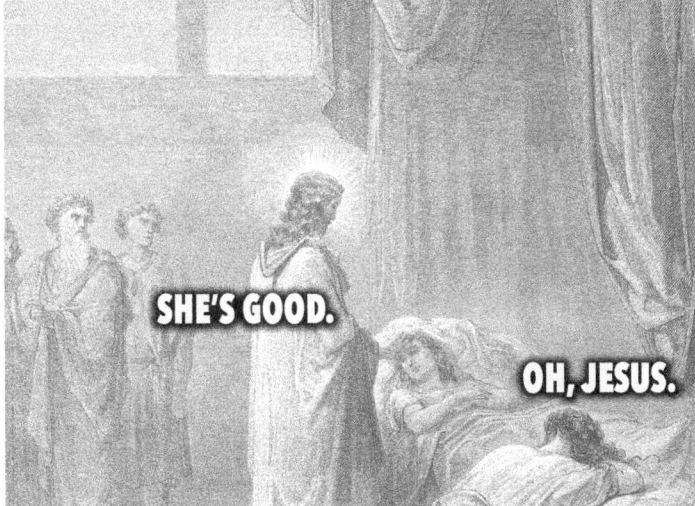

HELP HER, JESUS, HER SKIN IS COVERED IN HIVES.
IS IT LEPROSY?
LET'S NOT MAKE ANY RASH DECISIONS.

THAT'S IT, WE'RE SKIPPING CHRISTMAS THIS YEAR.

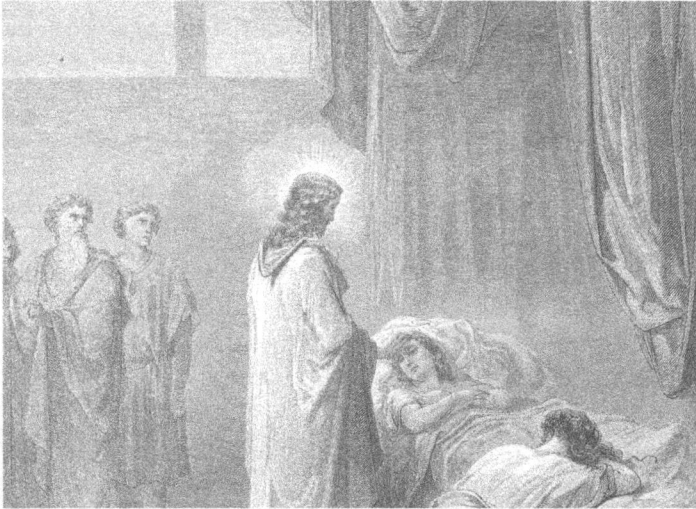

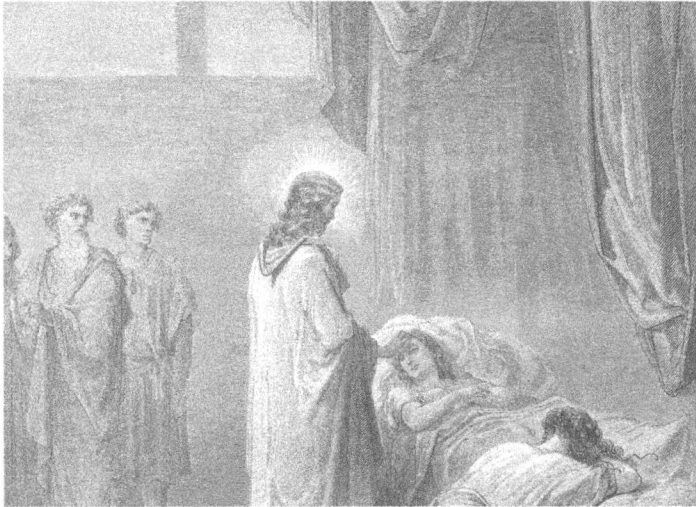

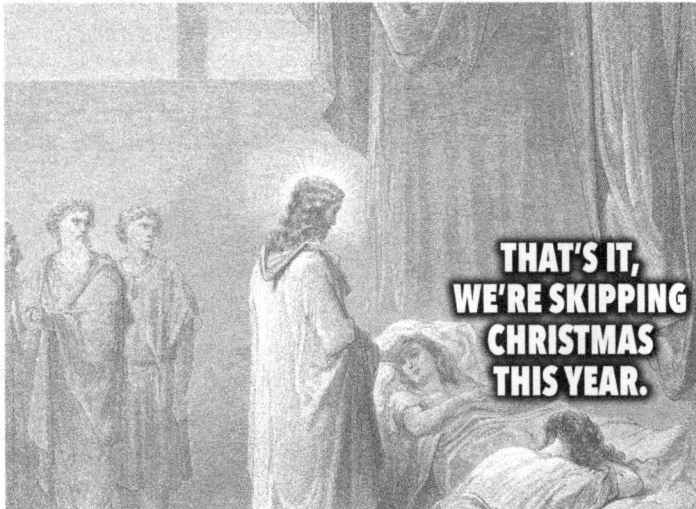

SO I HEAR YOU LOVE GARDENING?
YEP, FROM MY HEAD TO-MA-TOES

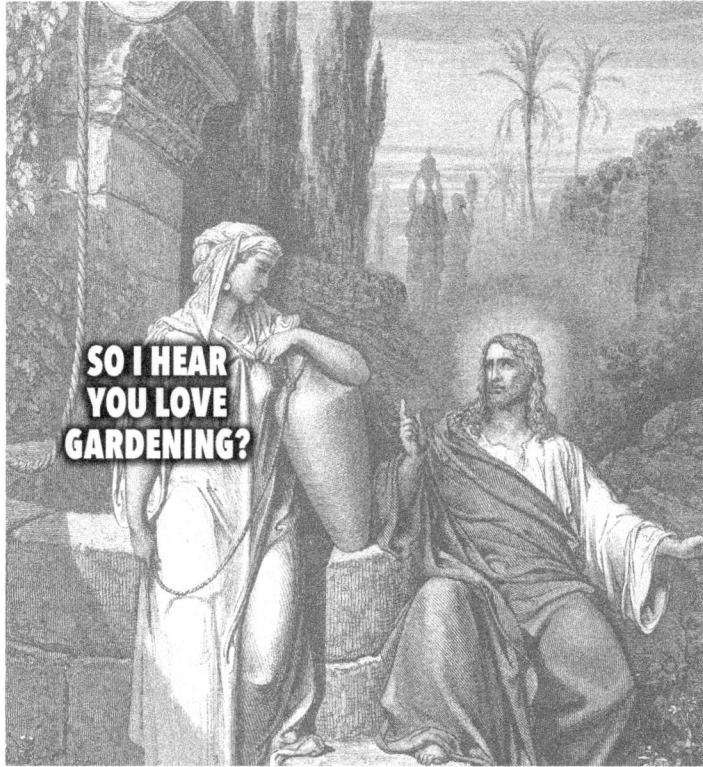

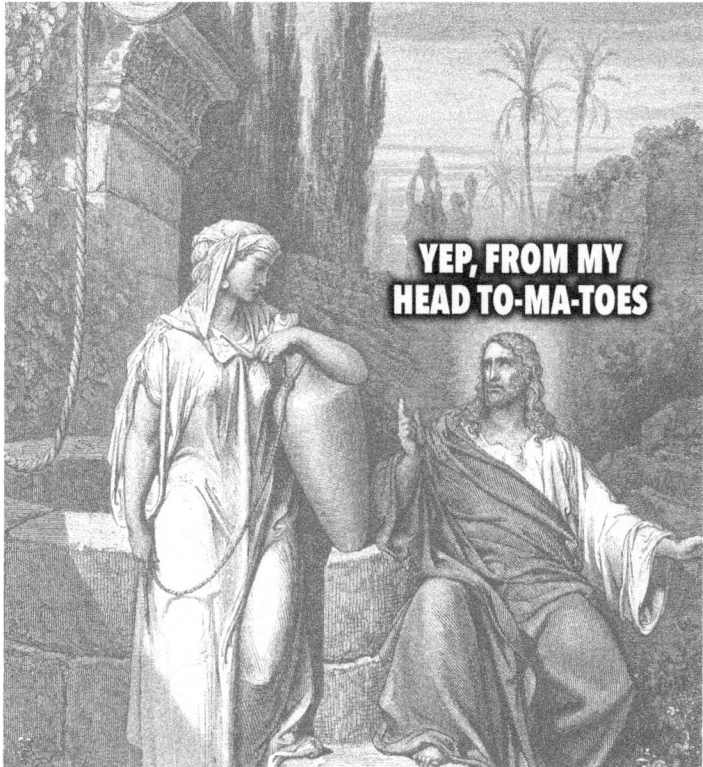

SEE, THE PROBLEM IS... YOU THINK THAT'S FUNNY.

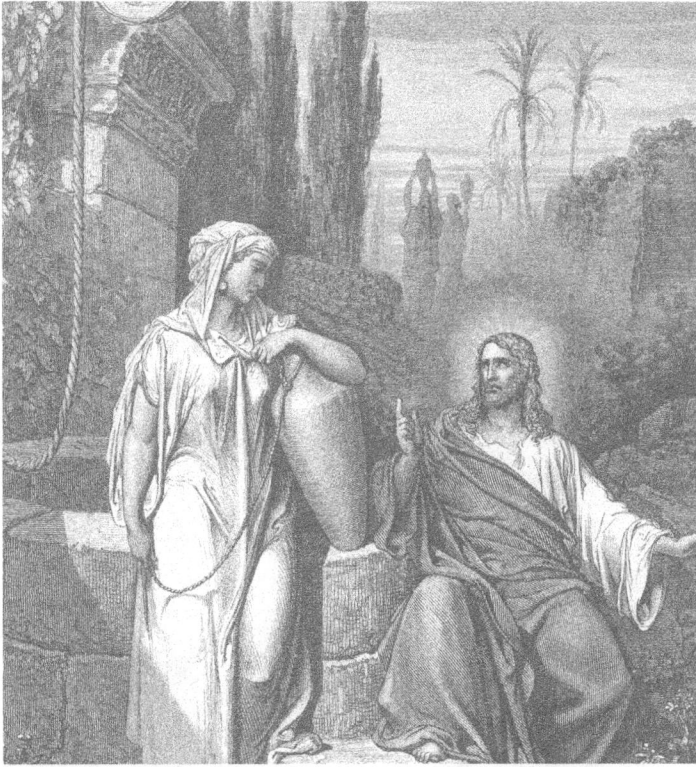

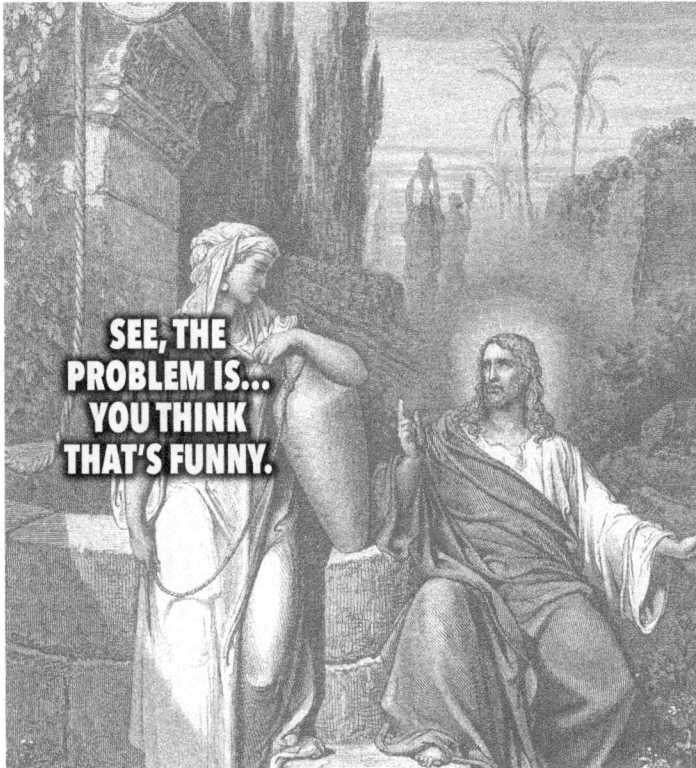

THIS IS GOOD, BUT MOSES MAKES THE BEST COFFEE I EVER TASTED.
HOW DOES HE MAKE IT?
HEBREWS IT

SERIOUSLY, PETER,
YOU DIDN'T SEE
THAT ONE COMING?

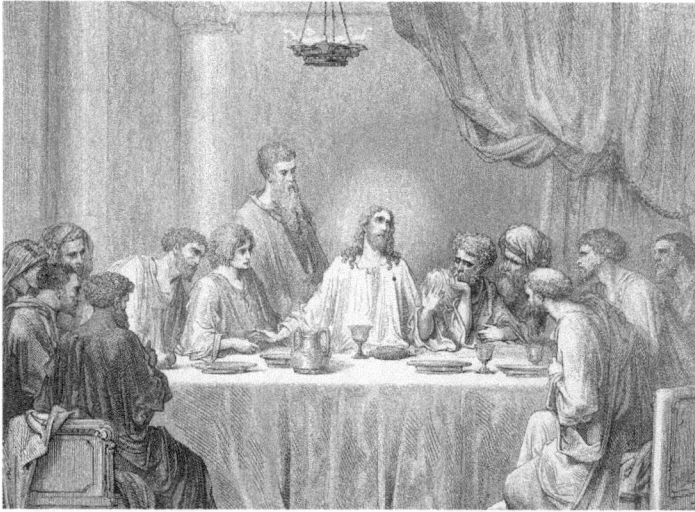

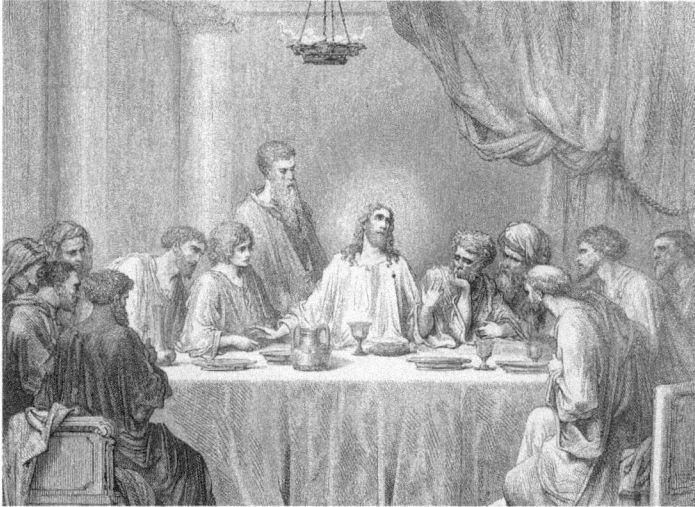

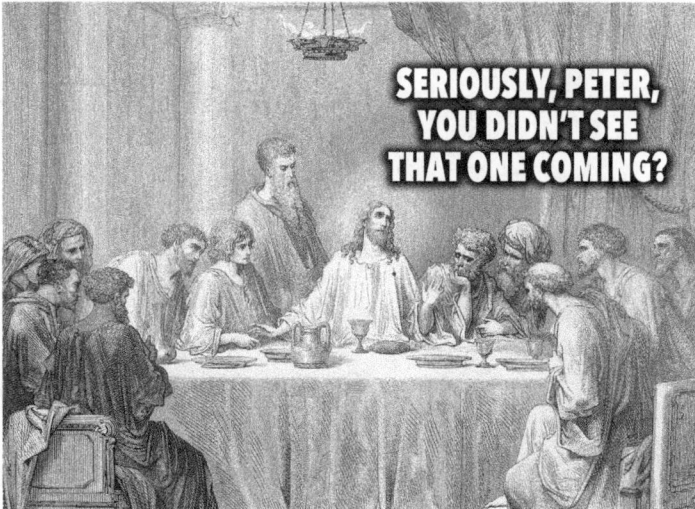

JESUS, YOU SHOULD JOIN US FOR LUNCH AT SUBWAY NEXT WEEK.
LEAVE ME ALONE, JUDAS.
WE'RE HAVING HEROES ON THE THIRD DAY.

HE-ROSE, JESUS.

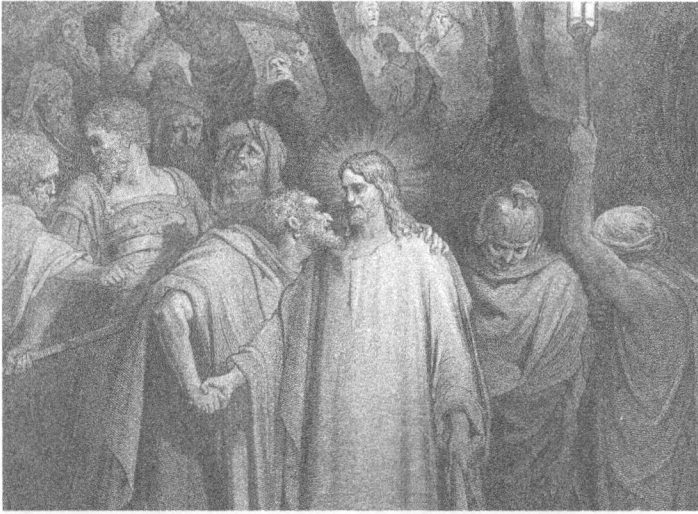

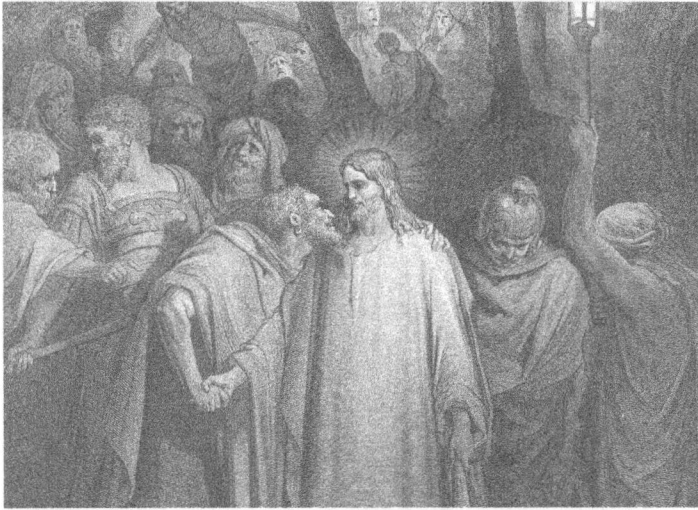

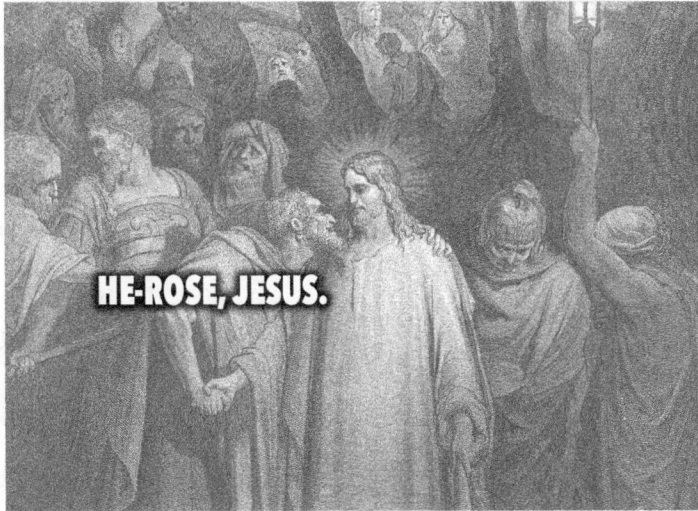

JESUS, YOUR DISCIPLES ARE EATING THE GRAPES RIGHT OFF THE VINE!
EEEEK, RUN!!! MAN EATING PLANTS!!!

JESUS, DO YOU EVER QUIT?

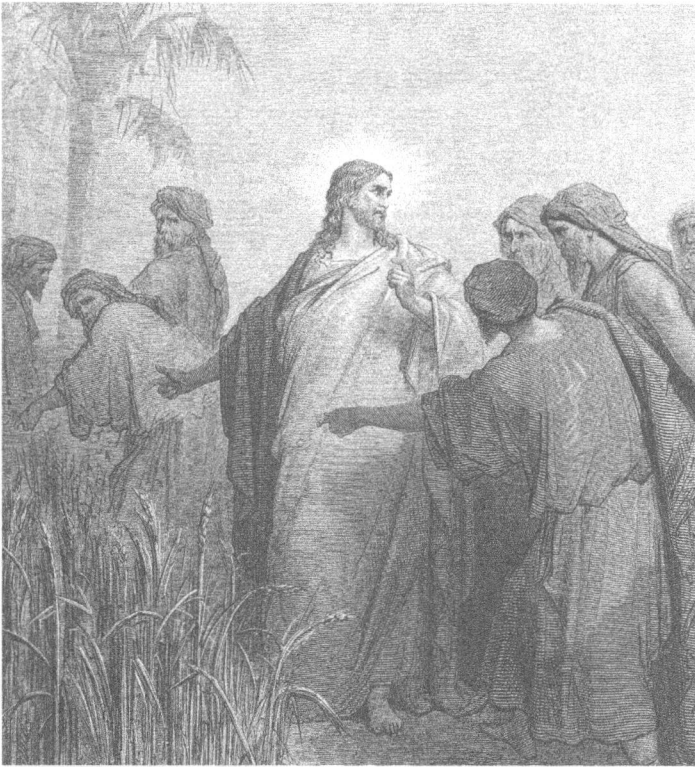

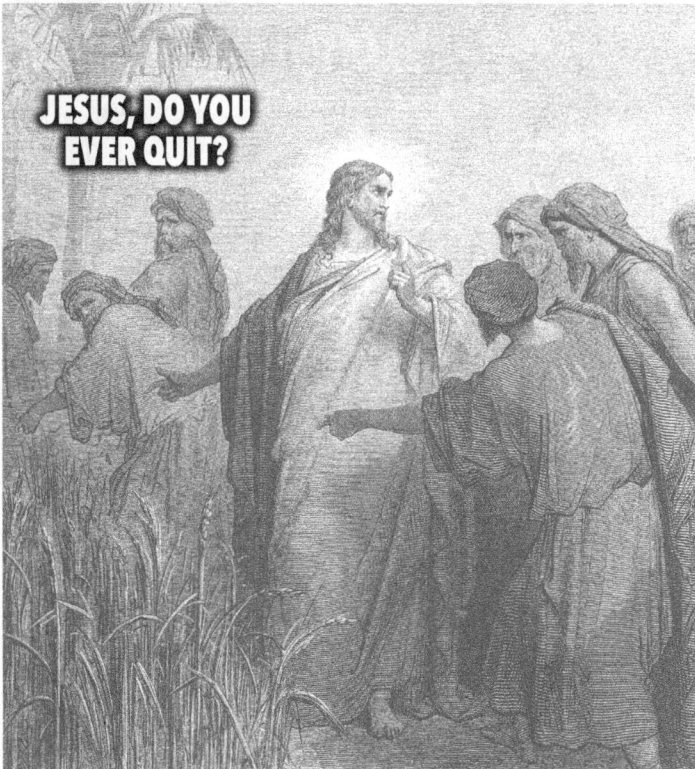

HEY JESUS, HOW IS YOUR STEAK?
SAVIORY

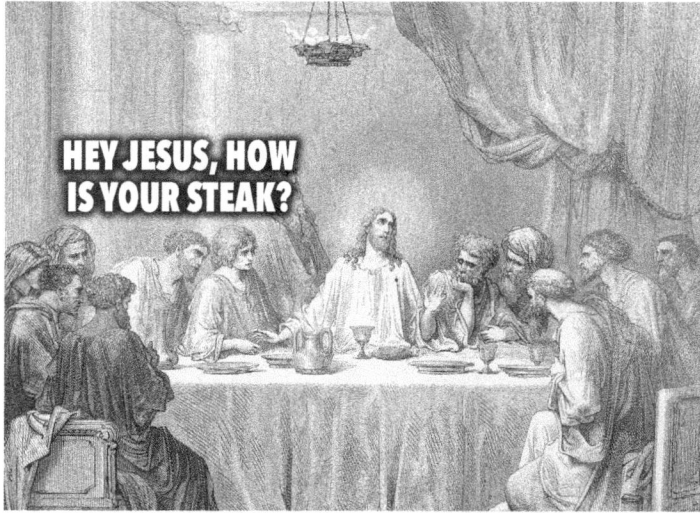

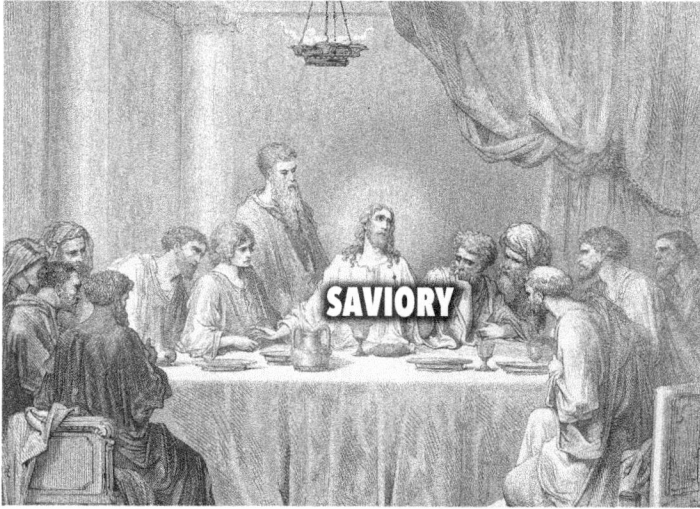

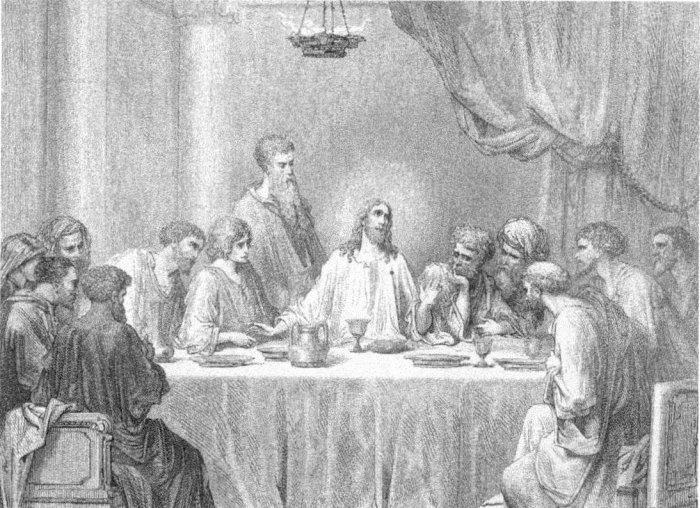

AW, CRAP, I JUST GOT THAT ONE.

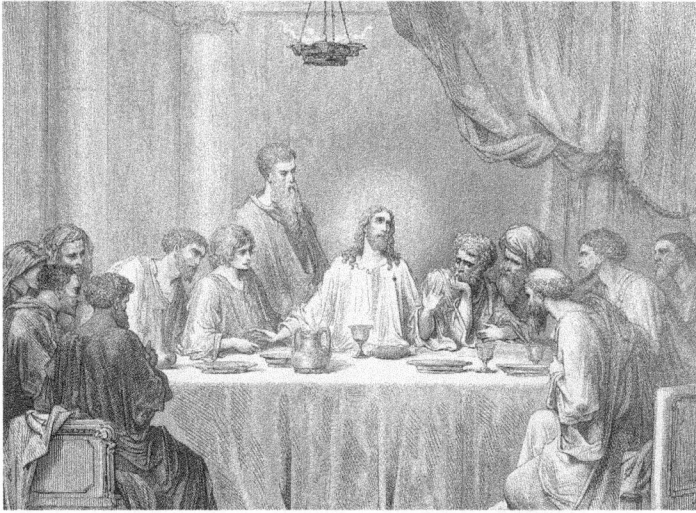

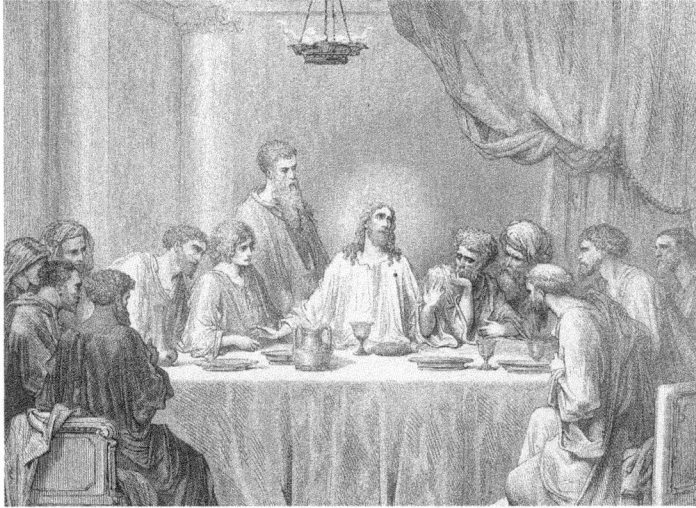

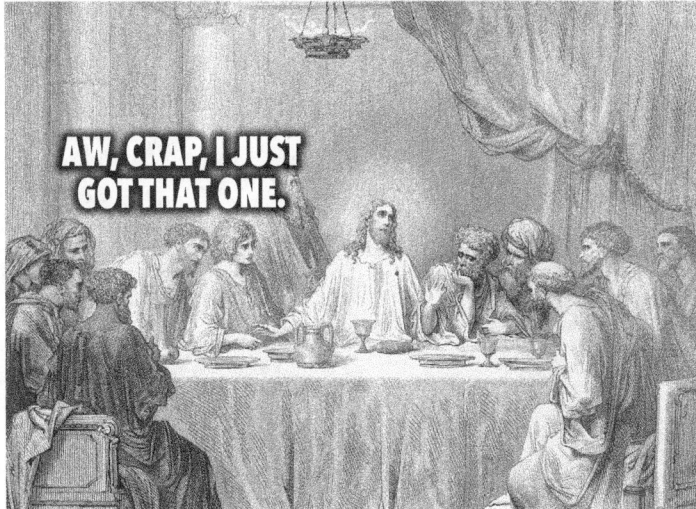

JESUS, WE'RE BEING ATTACKED BY A HORDE OF CIRCUS PERFORMERS...
WHAT SHOULD WE DO?
GO FOR THE JUGGULAR

the funniest guy in the room

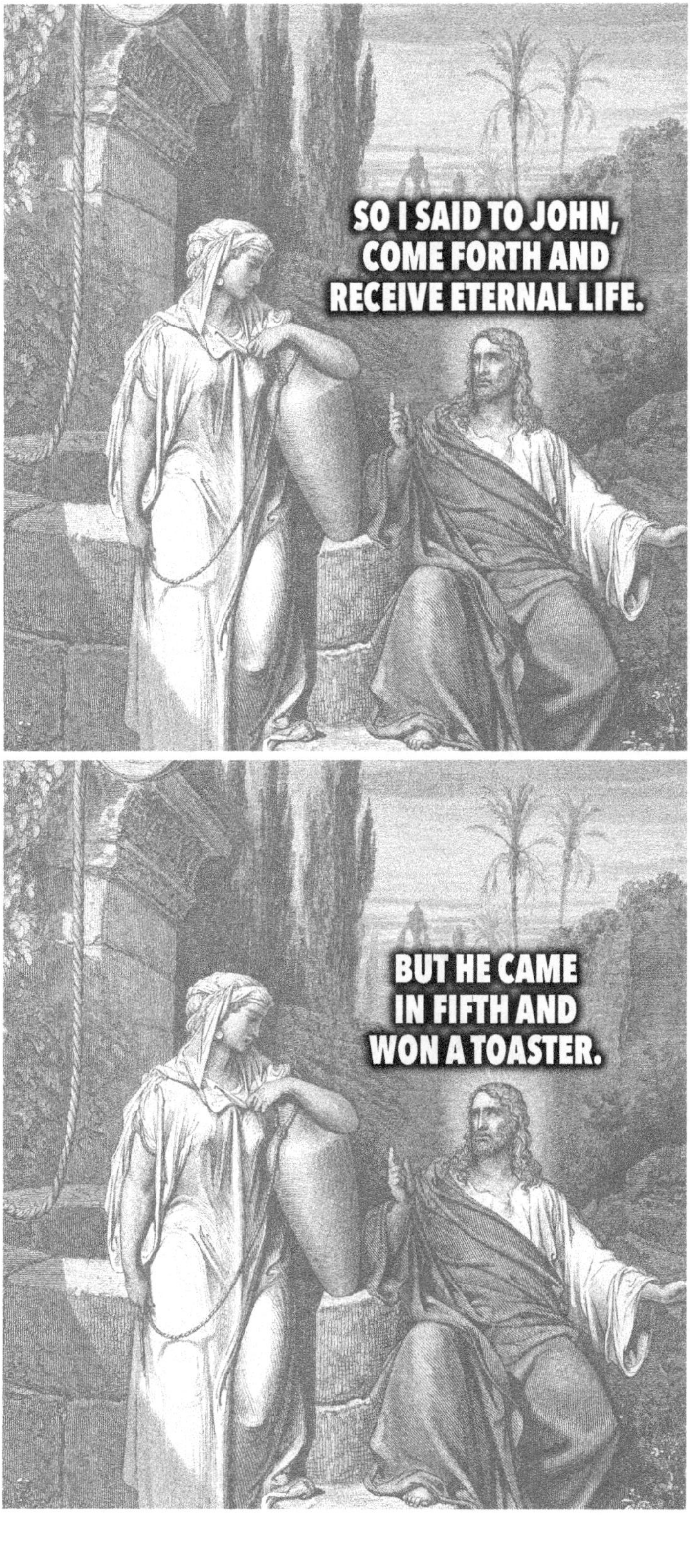
SO I SAID TO JOHN, COME FORTH AND RECEIVE ETERNAL LIFE.
BUT HE CAME IN FIFTH AND WON A TOASTER.

YEAH, DO THESE
LINES WORK WITH
THE JUDEAN WOMAN?

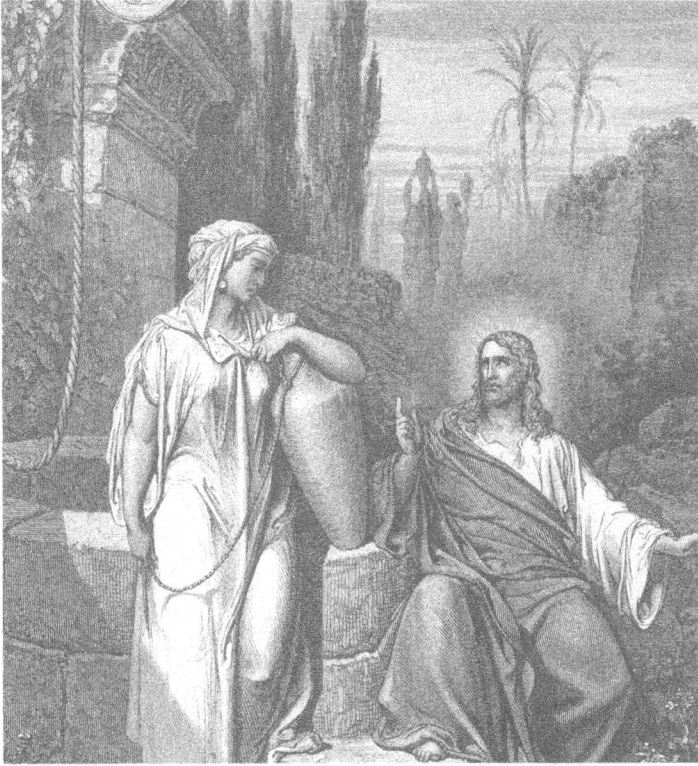

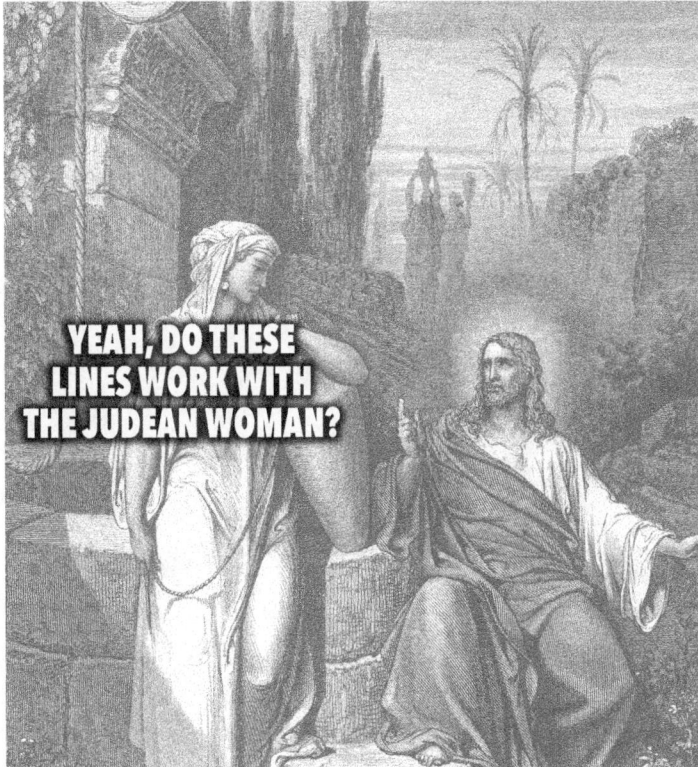

HEY, PETER, HOW MANY TICKLES DOES IT TAKE TO MAKE AN OCTOPUS LAUGH?
NOW IS NOT THE TIME, JESUS.
TEN. TEN-TICKLES.

THAT'S IT.
I'M LEAVING.

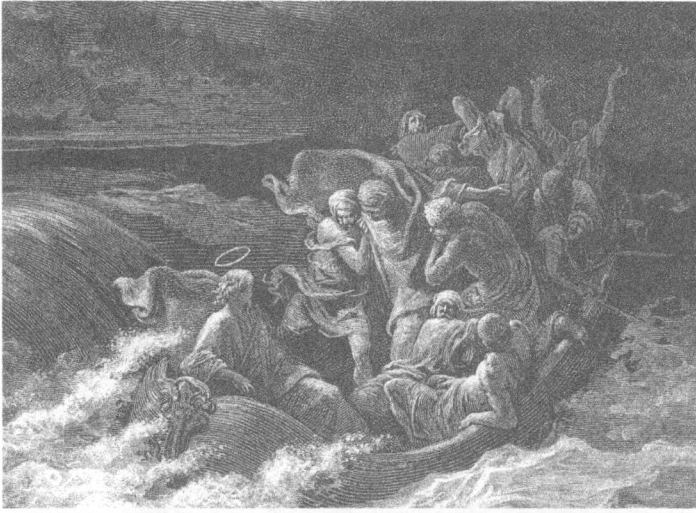

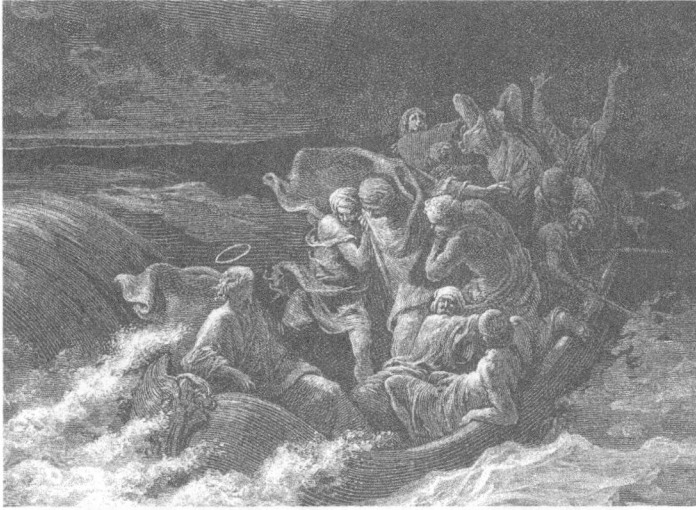

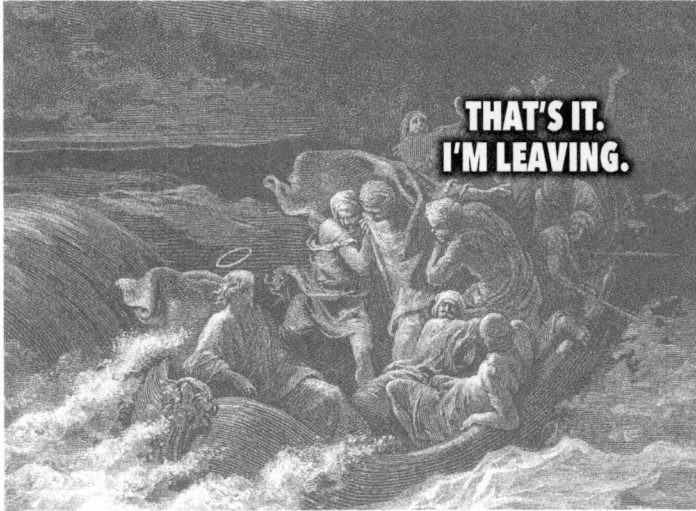

HEY, JESUS, WHY DID THE CHICKEN CROSS THE ROAD?
WHY?
TO GET TO THE UGLY GUY'S HOUSE.
KNOCK KNOCK
WHO'S THERE?

THE CHICKEN
IT'S THE CHICKEN, JESUS. HE'S AT YOUR HOUSE.

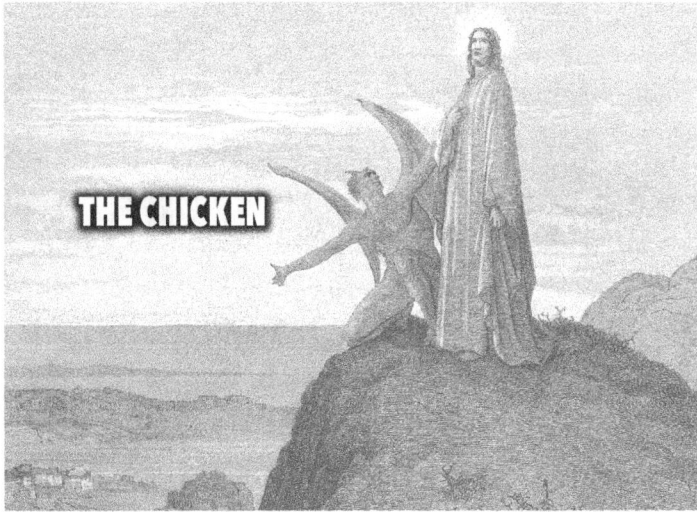

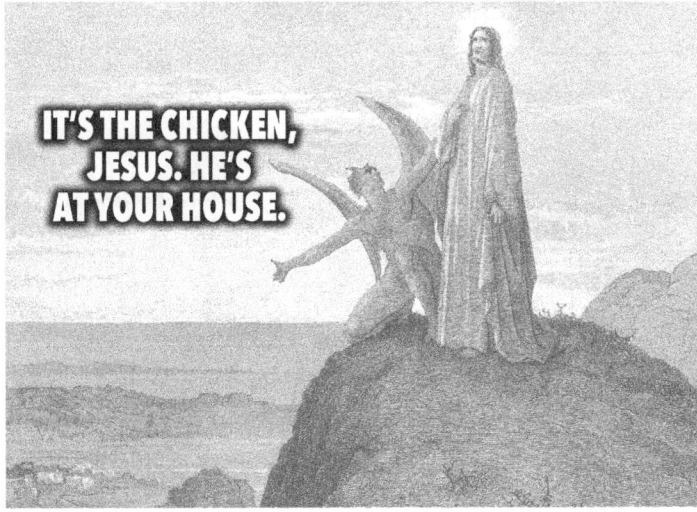

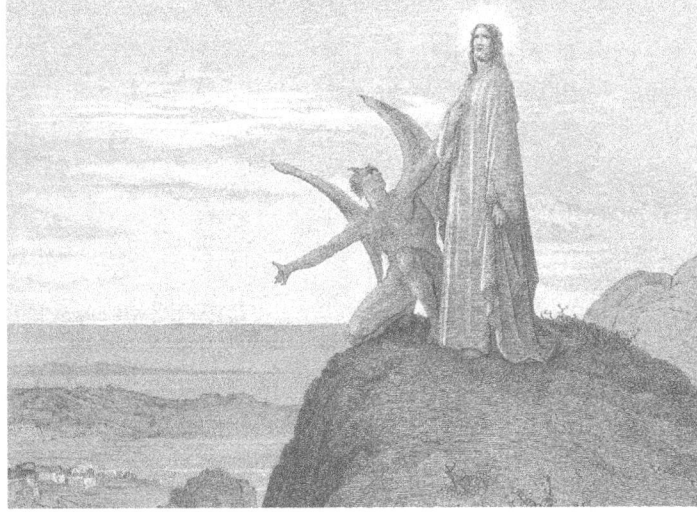

KNOCK KNOCK
WHO'S THERE?
EUROPE
EUROPE WHO?

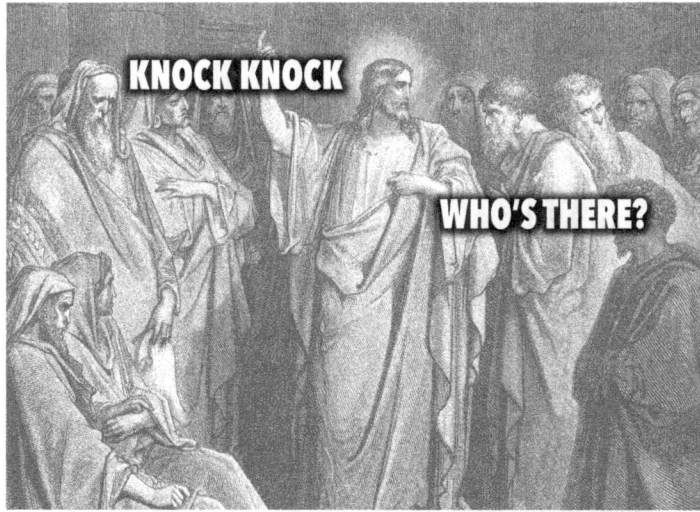

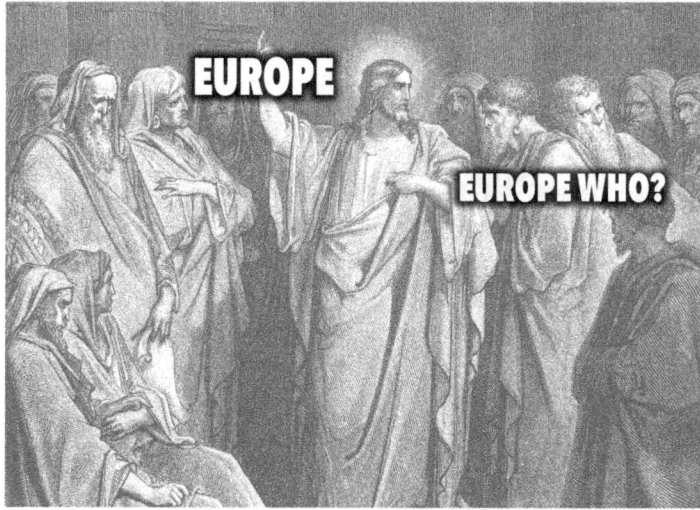

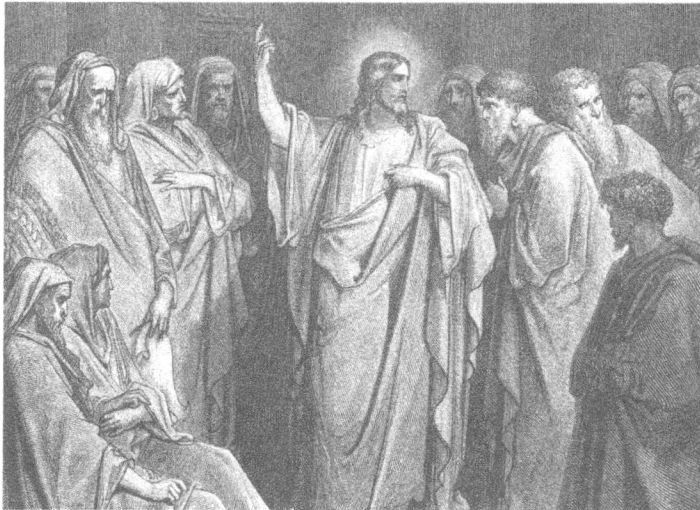

NO YOU'RE A POO!!

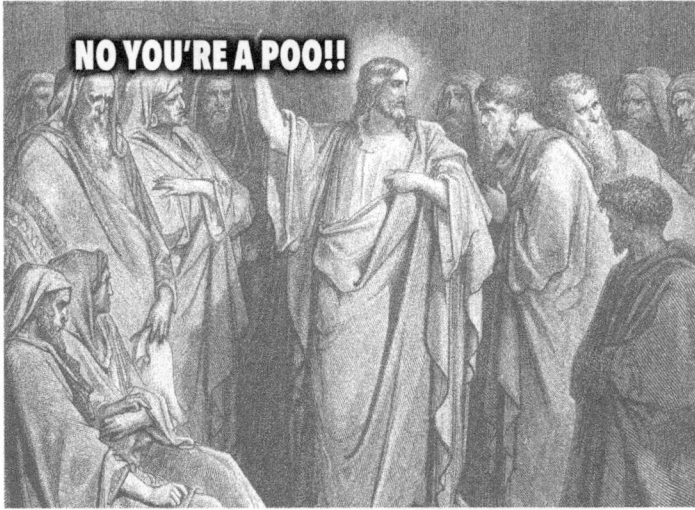

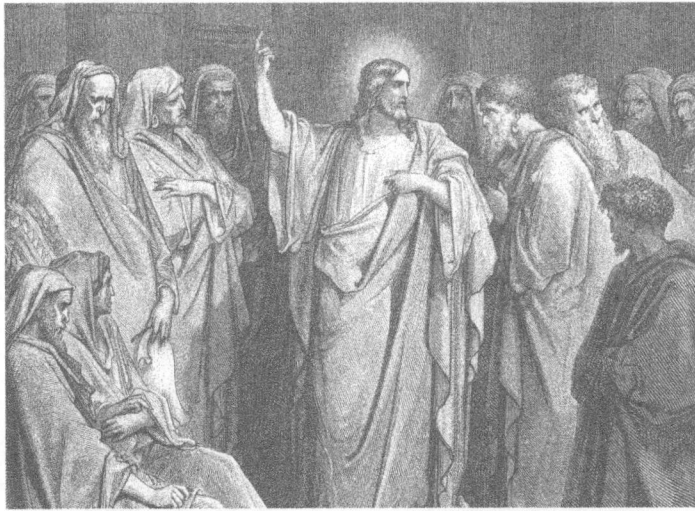

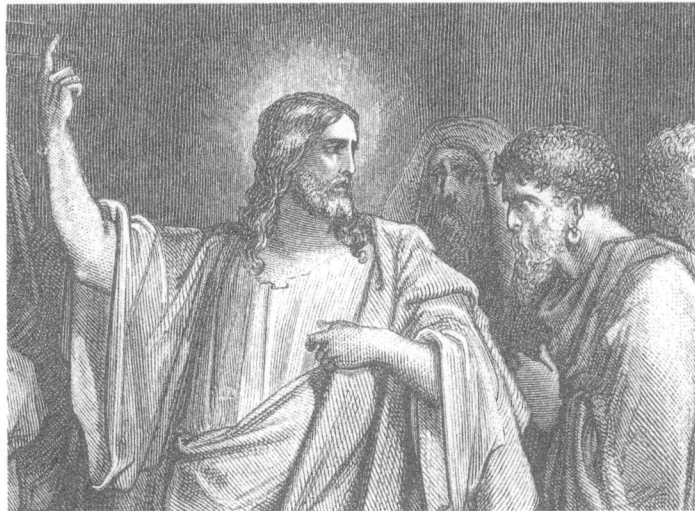

JESUS, CONDEMN HER. SHE IS UNCLEAN!
WHAT DO YOU CALL A BIG PILE OF KITTENS?

A MEOWTAIN.
UNCLEAN! UNCLEAN!

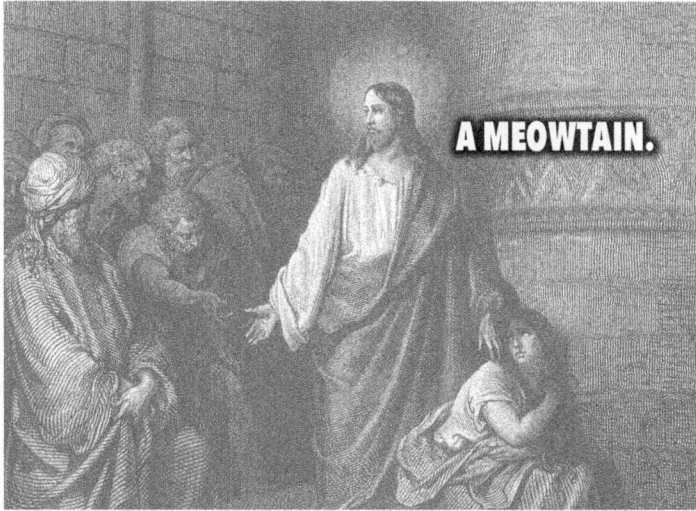

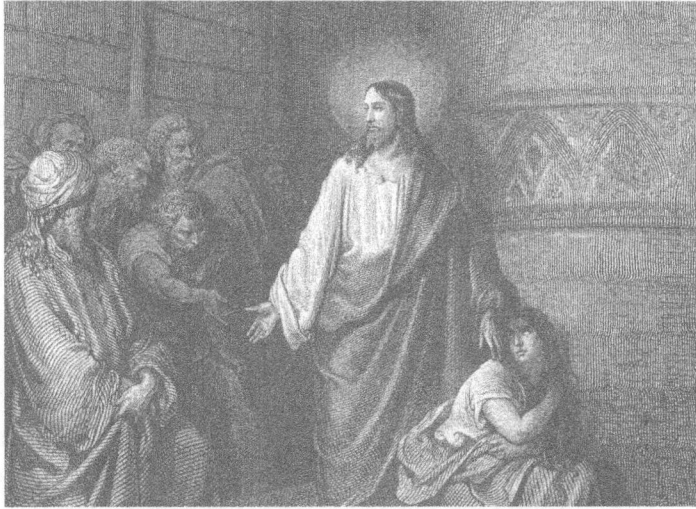

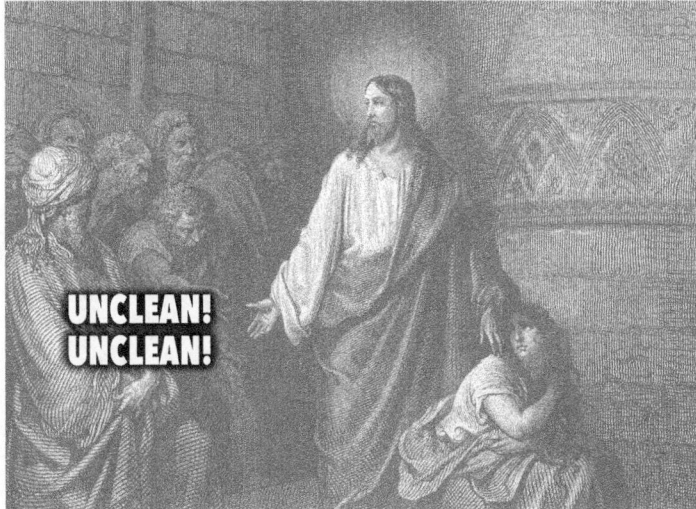

SEE, I JUST STEPPED ON THIS GRAPE. POOR LITTLE GUY.
DID IT SAY ANYTHING?

NO. IT JUST GAVE
A LITTLE WHINE.

JESUS, WHAT KIND OF MEAT IS THIS?
BABY WOOKIE.
HOW DO YOU KNOW?

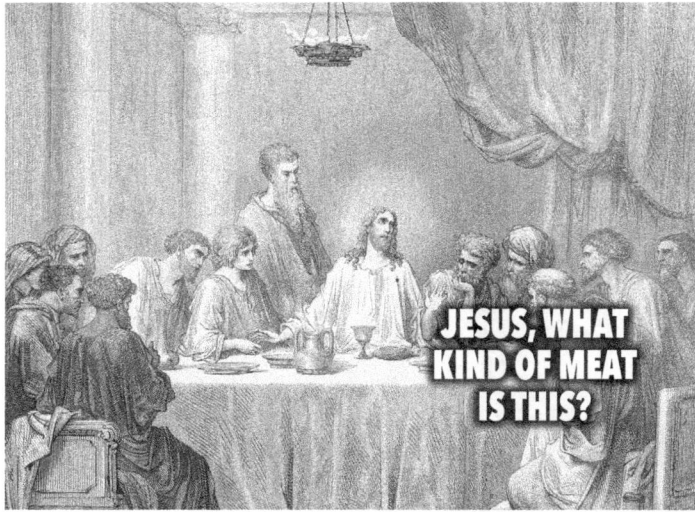

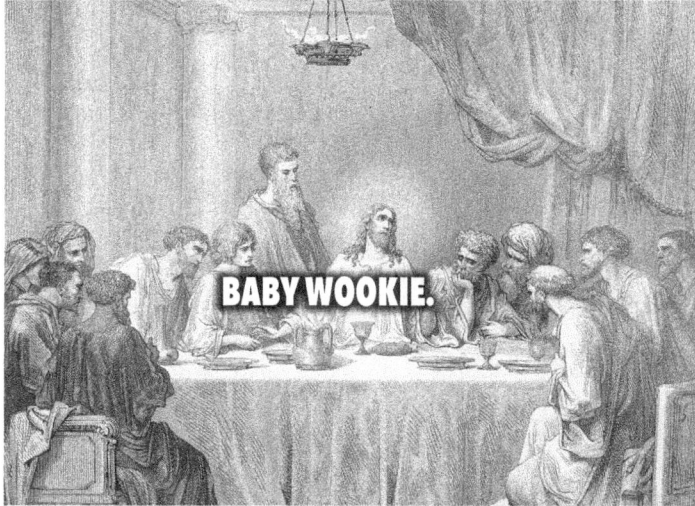

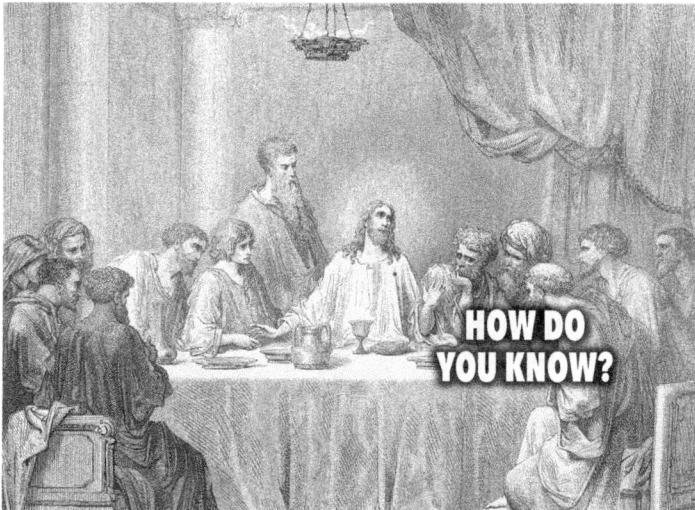

IT'S A LITTLE CHEWIE.
JESUS, GEORGE LUCAS' LAWYERS ARE ON THE PHONE.

JESUS, HEAL HIM.
HE CAN'T SEE HIS FRIENDS.
WHY? IS
HE MARRIED?

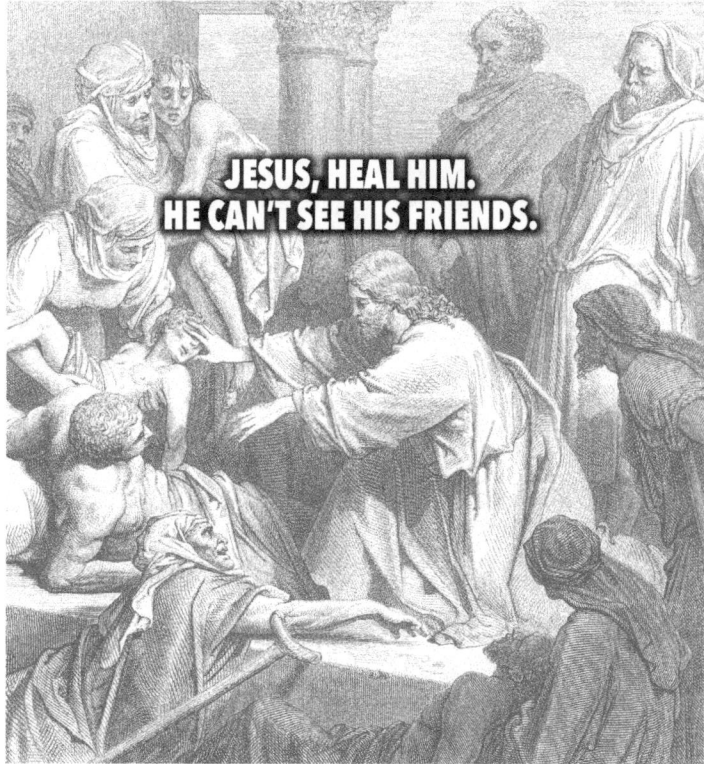

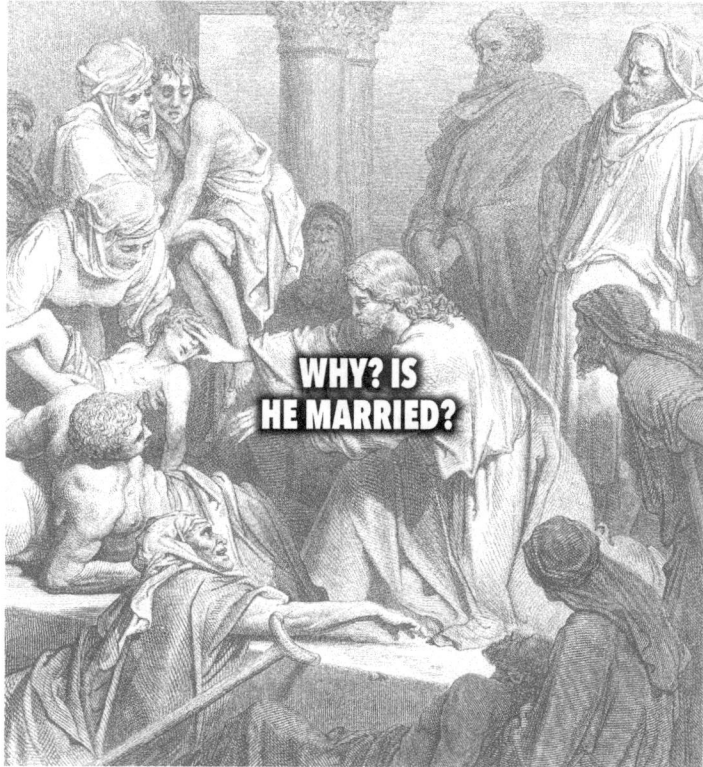

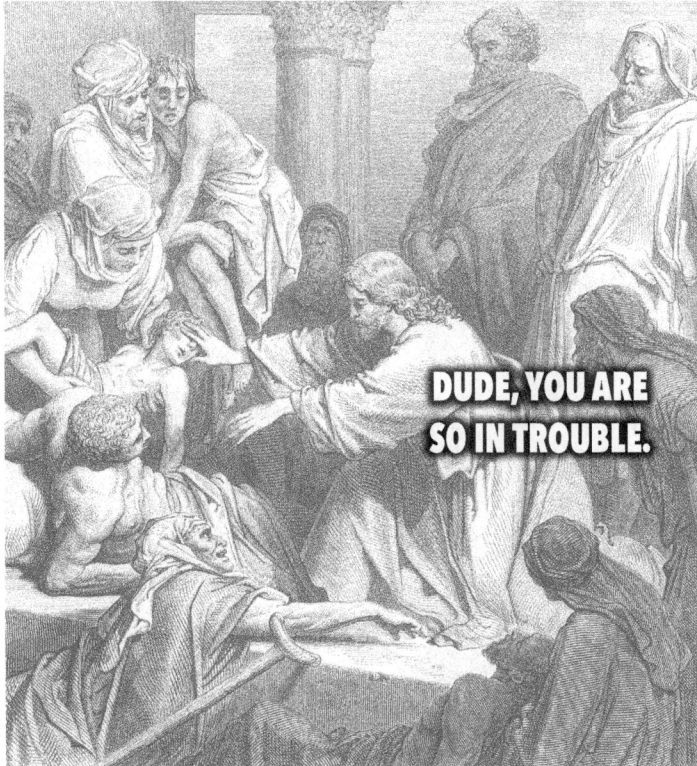

DUDE, YOU ARE
SO IN TROUBLE.

HEY, JESUS, WHAT'S
THE DIFFERENCE BETWEEN
ROAST BEEF AND PEA SOUP?
ANYBODY CAN
ROAST BEEF.
HEH.

SHUT UP. YOU CAN NOT...
NOT AS EASY AS WATER INTO WINE BUT....

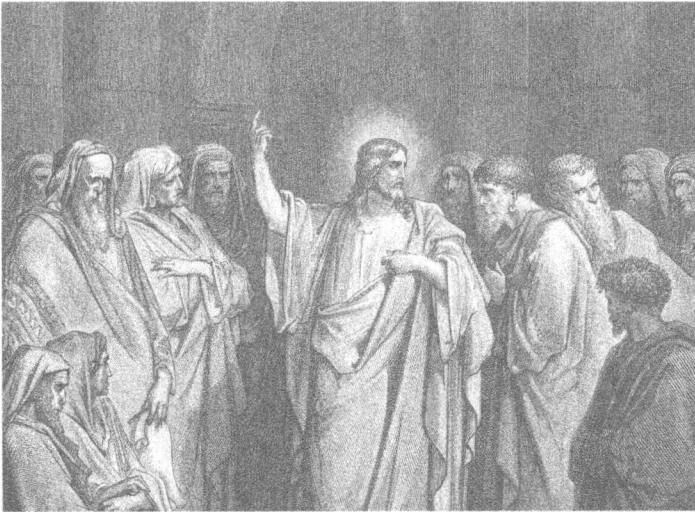

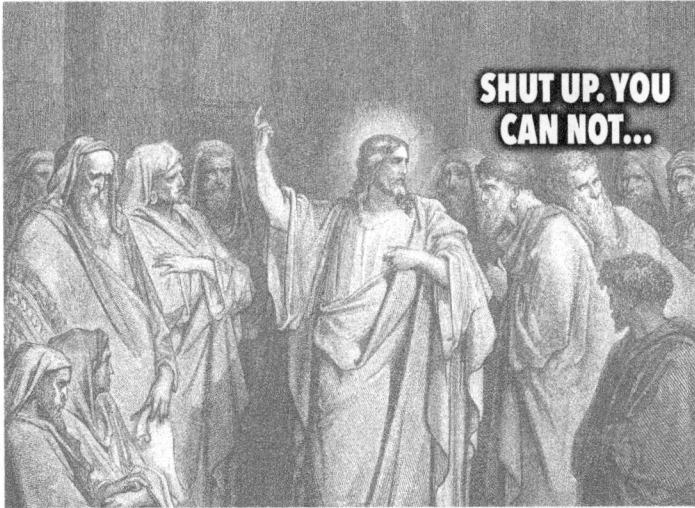

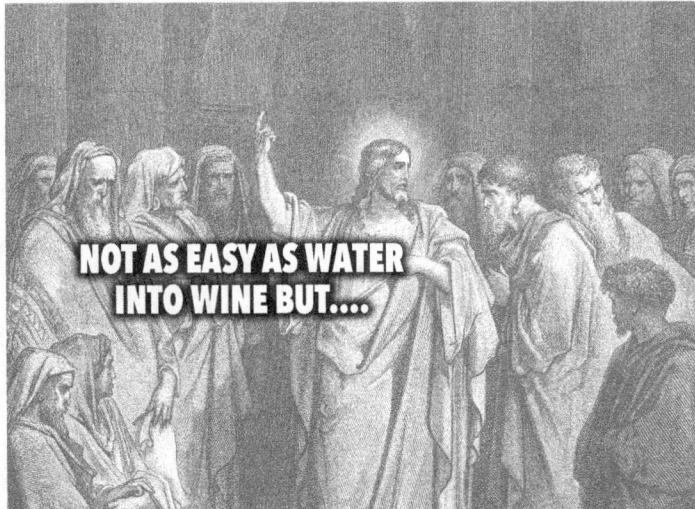

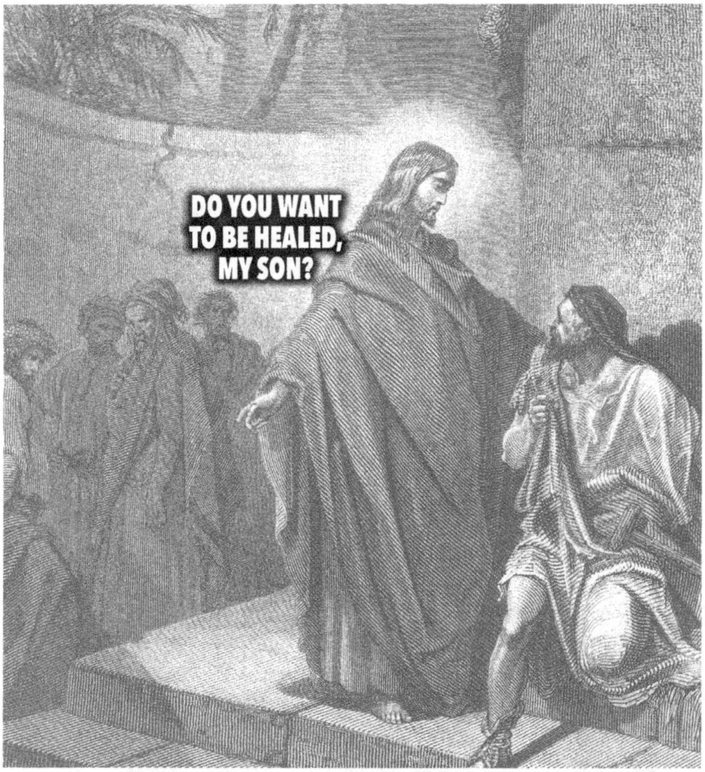
DO YOU WANT TO BE HEALED, MY SON?

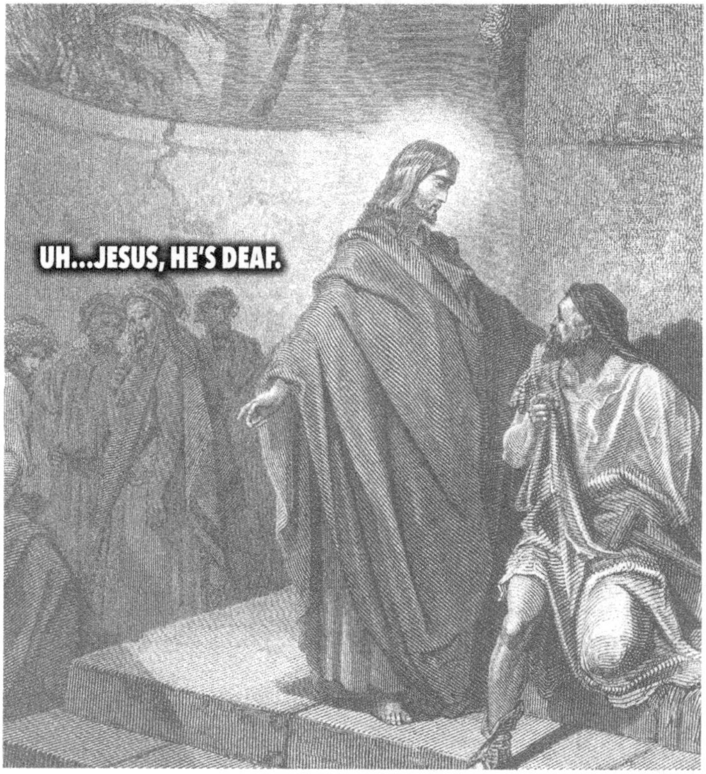
UH...JESUS, HE'S DEAF.

OH....
DO YOU WANT TO BE HEALED MY SON??!!

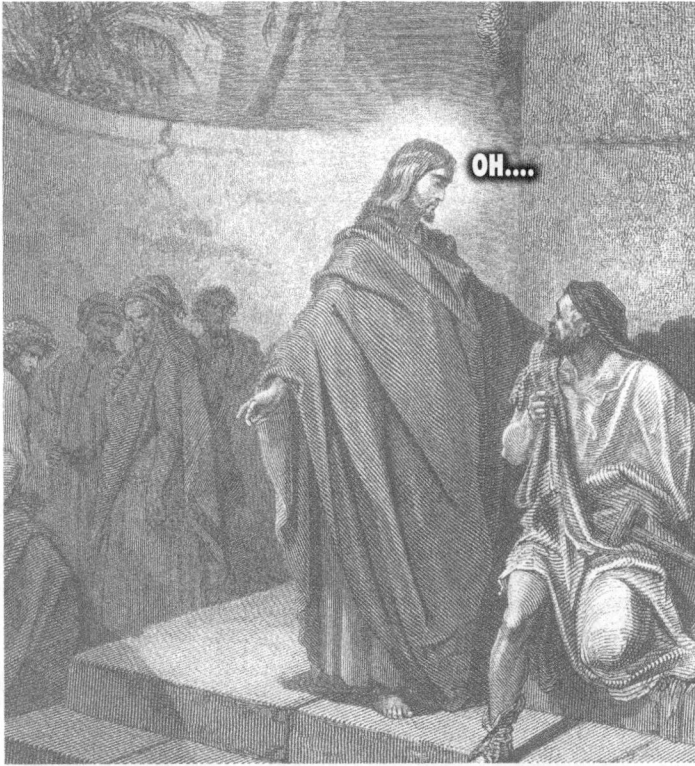

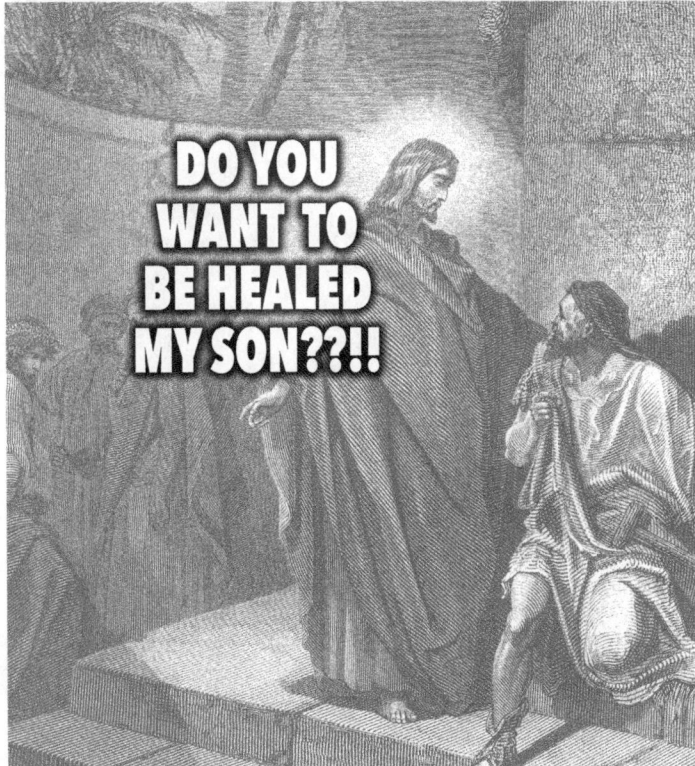

HEY PETER, WHAT'S BRUCE LEE'S FAVORITE BEVERAGE?
WHO?
WAAAATAHHH!

WHO?

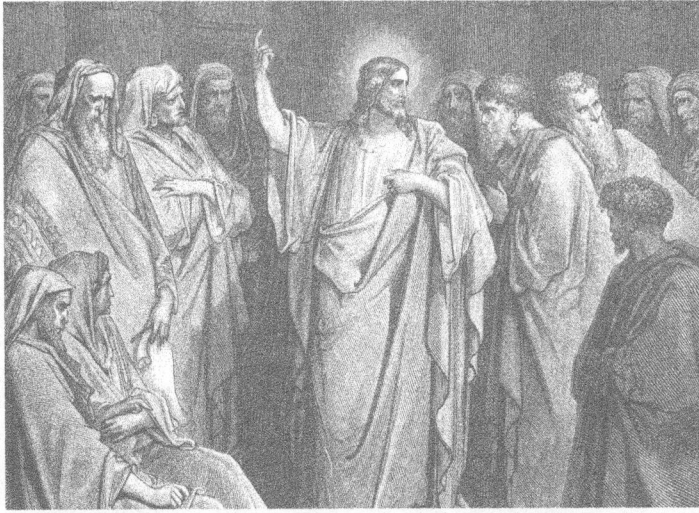

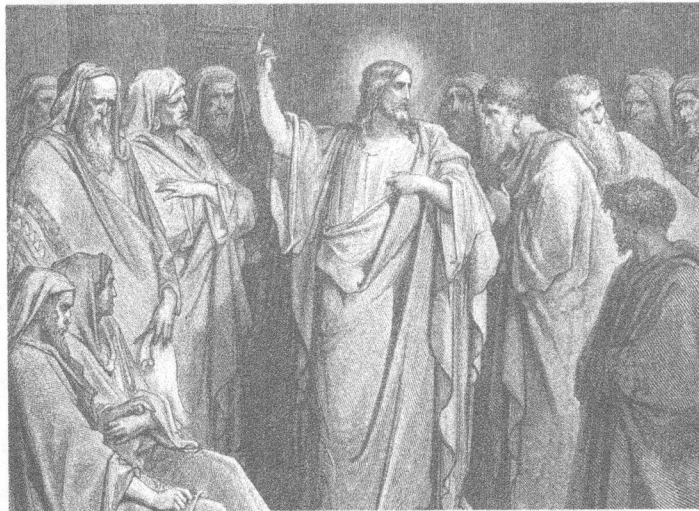

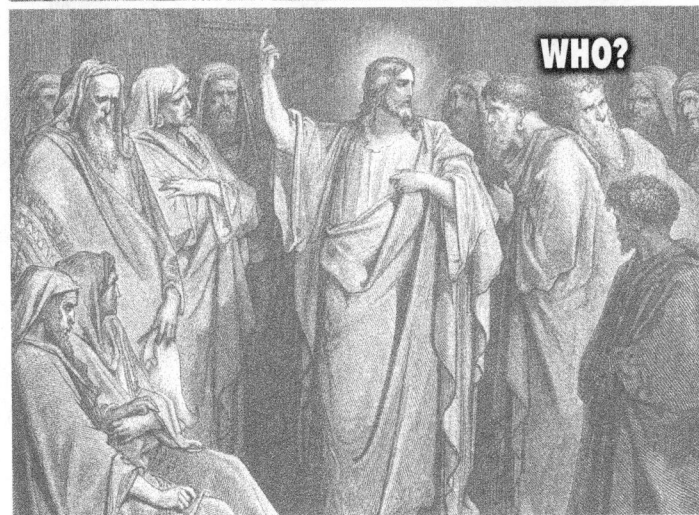

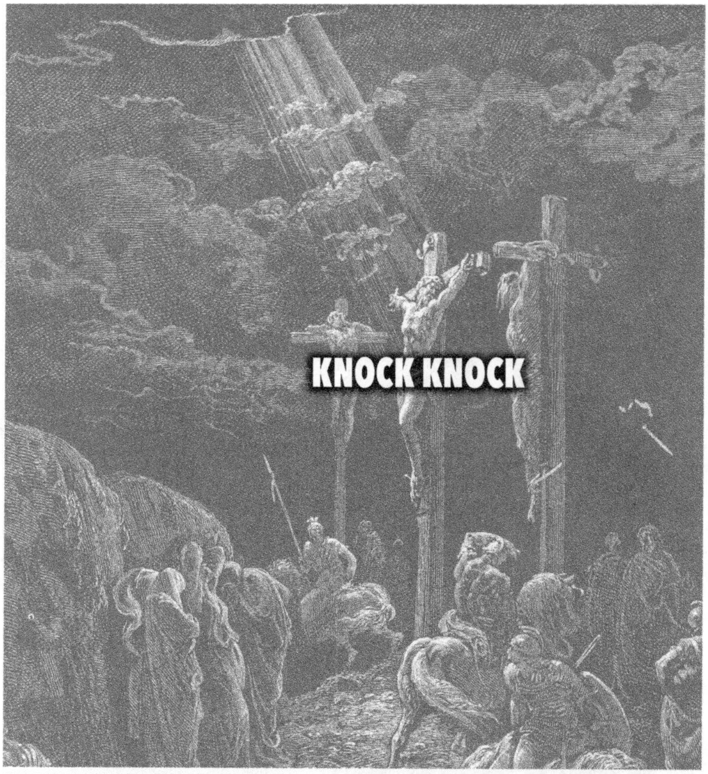
KNOCK KNOCK

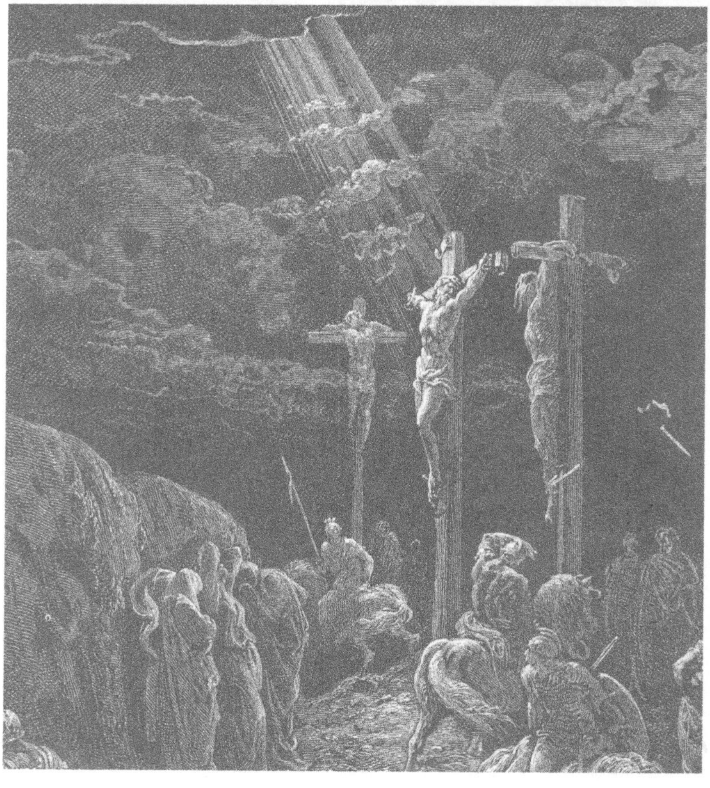

WHO'S THERE?

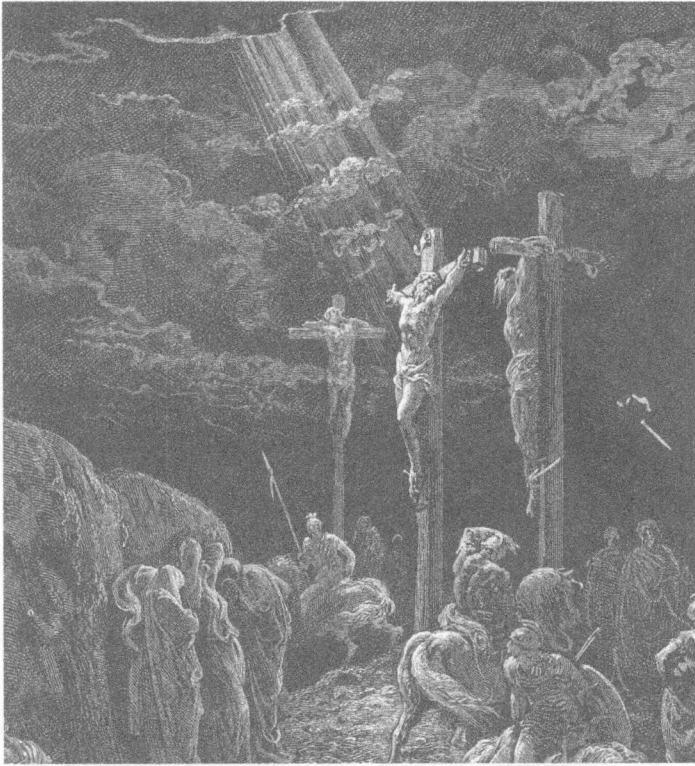

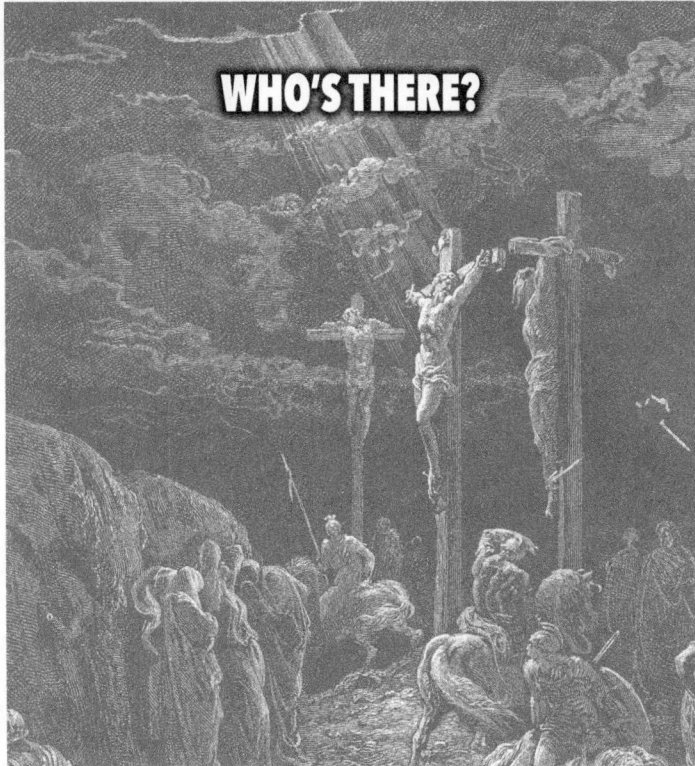

www.ingramcontent.com/pod-product-compliance
Lightning Source LLC
Chambersburg PA
CBHW081419090426
42738CB00017B/3419